Crystal Spirit—the Next Step on the Frontier of Change

Crystal Spirit is the book that thousands of people have asked for after reading the immensely popular *Crystal Power* by Michael G. Smith. *Crystal Spirit* contains answers to questions about crystals that are not available anywhere else, and it has many new and exciting crystal tools that are economical and easy to build and use.

Crystal Spirit explores a wide area of the crystal world, including:

- Crystals of the ancient past
- Crystal healing rods
- Crystal power rods
- Crystal dowsing tools
- Crystal pyramid devices
- Car crystals
- Crystal psionic black box computer machines
- Crystal wands and crystal hands for Ki and Chi work

The book ends with the introduction of the new Crystal Pipe, which is based on traditional Native American practices and the science of Universal Energy. All these crystal devices are accompanied by complete instructions and detailed diagrams for constructing them.

Now that the fad appeal of crystals has worn off, we can use crystals to experience the deeper essence of ourselves—to facilitate our self-awareness, self-growth, and self-understanding. As we work with crystals, we radiate the kind of energy that makes a better world. We are all part of Crystal Spirit.

About the Author

Michael Smith was born in Great Bend, Kansas on March 9, 1947 and grew up on a Kansas farm/ranch near where he was born. He has studied ancient knowledge for 25 years. Some of that time was spent with the Bear Tribe Medicine Society, where he was first introduced to quartz crystals by Sun Bear, the Medicine Man. This inspired Michael to invent the crystal healing rod and the crystal headband 15 years ago. He has been working with crystals constantly since that time. He is the inventor of over one hundred crystal tools, many of which are now in use in the United States and dozens of other countries around the world.

While working on this book with Melinda J. Westhorp, *Crystal Spirit* became a work of love. Michael and Melinda were married during the Harmonic Convergence of 1987. They have a lot in common, since they share the same birthday, March 9th. Melinda is also a writer, currently working on an inspired novel of the New Age.

To Write to the Author

We cannot guarantee that every letter written to the author can be answered, but all will be forwarded. Both the author and the publisher appreciate hearing from readers, learning of your enjoyment and benefit from this book. Llewellyn also publishes a bi-monthly news magazine with news and reviews of practical esoteric studies and articles helpful to the student. Some readers' questions and comments to the author may be answered through this magazine's columns if permission to do so is included in the original letter. The author sometimes participates in seminars and workshops, and dates and places are announced in *The Llewellyn New Times*. To write to the author, or to ask a question, write to:

Michael G. Smith
c/o THE LLEWELLYN NEW TIMES
P.O. Box 64383-726, St. Paul, MN 55164-0383, U.S.A.

Please enclose a self-addressed, stamped envelope for reply, or $1.00 to cover costs.

ABOUT LLEWELLYN'S NEW AGE PSI•TECH SERIES

Psychic Powers—we really understand very little about them. But, with an open mind, we have to admit the evidence that they do exist. We witness them in history, religion and myth, and we witness them all about us in both ordinary and extra-ordinary circumstances. We witness these amazing powers in psychic phenomena, radionics and psionics, in divination and dowsing, in healing and prophecy, and in miracles and mysteries of all kinds.

Over the whole history of humanity, these powers have been experienced and cultivated by shamans, magicians, witches and yogis, by holy (whole) men and women, and by people-in-need. Today, we also find them in the research laboratory and in the homes and offices of ordinary men and women seeking understanding of such phenomena and powers so that they can be directed and applied to self-improvement and attainment, *and for success.*

There are many *technologies* for developing and applying these little-known powers. But even when we lack under-standing of how something works, we can still find ways to apply it for our own benefit. Psychic Power lies dormant in everyone, and everyone—no matter who he or she is—can bring it out and use it. There are established technologies for psychic development and application, and there are simple "machines" (or interfaces) that can help develop and amplify your psychic powers.

In Llewellyn's Psi•Tech Series of books and tapes, we focus on these techniques and devices for tapping the many powers of the psyche, including those that join psyche and body, visible and invisible, life and Earth, humanity and cosmos. With this knowledge we seek better control over the personal environment, adding a new and significant resource in dealing with the problems of everyday living—*and a means to understand and control the invisible factors that shape energies and events at community and planetary levels.*

Other Books by Michael G. Smith
Crystal Power

Forthcoming Books
Crystal Warrior

Llewellyn's Psi•Tech Series

Crystal Spirit

by

Michael G. Smith

1990
Llewellyn Publications, Inc.
St. Paul, Minnesota, 55164-0383, U.S.A.

International Standard Book Number: 0-87542-726-X
Library of Congress Catalog Number: 89-77150

First Edition, 1990
First Printing, 1990

Library of Congress Cataloging-in-Publication Data

Smith, Michael G. (Michael Gary), 1947-
    Crystal spirit / Michael G. Smith.
        p. cm. — (Llewellyn's new age Psi-tech series)
    ISBN 0-87542-726-X
    1. Crystals-Miscellanea.   I. Title.   II. Series.
BF1442.C78S65 1990   89-77150
133.3'22—dc20   CIP

Cover Painting: Lissanne Lake
Illustrations: Christopher Wells
based on concepts by Michael Smith

Produced by Llewellyn Publications
Typography and Art property of Chester-Kent, Inc.

Published by
LLEWELLYN PUBLICATIONS
A Division of Llewellyn Worldwide, Ltd.
P.O. Box 64383
St. Paul, MN 55164-0383, U.S.A.

Printed in the United States of America

*Dedicated to the people
who go beyond words, thoughts
and emotions
to the energy experience of being.*

Special thanks
to
Melinda J. Westhorp
for her help and inspiration,
and to Denzil Wiggins and the crew at the
Red and Green Mineral Shop
7595 W. Florida Avenue
Lakewood, Colorado 80226

Contents

Foreword

"Crystals are for people who love the Earth."

The Crystal Earth Network is in place and growing at a tremendous pace. There is a common bond of interest in crystals worldwide that lets us all share in the growing connection of the Spirit as one human family on Earth. People of both sexes and of all ages, nationalities, religions, and races have expressed a kinship with each other through crystals. Lapis, rose quartz, adventurine, pipestone and others are being cut, polished and shaped into crystal forms for jewelry and healing stones. There is something big going on here!

Traditional Earth people in many countries have been using and wearing crystals throughout history in healing and religious practices. In the last decade crystals have spread through the mainstream of societies in many countries. At first it may have been the collectors of "pretty rocks," the metaphysical seekers, and the scientists studying subatomic particle physics who were interested in crystals. Now it appears that everybody is being attracted to crystals for almost as many reasons as there are people.

We expect to find crystals being used by traditional Earth healers and medicine people such as astrologers, psychics, students of magic and ancient science, and even physicists. But now people in all areas of life are acquiring, wearing and using crystals: construction workers, housewives, soldiers, computer programmers, grandmothers, gardeners, clerks, mechanics, teachers, musicians, painters and many more all have their crystals. We even find that crystals and crystal books are being smuggled into countries where there is government censorship. In these areas, the underground and black market provide the books and crystals that people want.

This popularity of crystals among so many people forms a planet-wide connection of energy in the spirit of peace. Humanity is being united in mind and spirit. The Crystal Revolution has been an individual inner experience so far, but this is ready to change as the spirit of peace, balance and harmony progresses to the expression of outward manifestation.

Experience has taught us not to attack the fear and aggression in our world directly, because that only adds energy to it and creates more of the same thing. Fear and aggression can, however, be phased out as they're replaced by beneficial expressions of joy and peace. The way we can tell that the outward Crystal Revolution is ready to happen is by knowing that the inner Crystal Revolution is already happening now as people wear and use crystals. Crystal workers have already prepared the way and built the foundation of a New World for a New Age.

Universal Planetary Consciousness is a term that describes the spiritual impetus underlying the Crystal Revolution. Throughout the Earth Mother's geological history the mineral kingdom's crystals have remained concentrated in pockets and veins deep within the Earth where they grew. These deposits of crystals acted as energy centers for the Earth's giant life force generator. The Earth Mother, conscious being that she is, has decided to heal and rebalance herself. Some of the energy information for this process came from a larger being that our planet is a part of—the Universe. The same spirit of healing is transmitted by the Universal Planetary Consciousness to and through crystals. It's also transmitted to humans, the vehicles of planetary healing. Humankind is responding by helping crystals move from their homes in concentrated pockets, and this joint venture is spreading crystals more evenly across the face of the globe.

The crystals, connected to the Universal Planetary Consciousness and each other with force lines of universal energy, are forming a new web of energy connections around the entire Earth. This new energy web, or grid pattern, is in harmony with healthy, peaceful lifeforms. This new energy grid is not compatible with greed, pollution, fear, war or aggression. We and the Earth are ready to help manifest a New Age on the planet that will phase out the destructive practices and forms that have characterized humanity's history. We, as individuals and as part of human consciousness, have a dream we share in common. We share the manifestation energy of mind and spirit through wearing and using the Earth Mother's crystals.

At almost any time in history, people have been waiting for a New Age. We are not waiting. We are bringing our New Age about with the support of the Universal Planetary Consciousness through crystal power. We are vehicles of universal energy using the Earth's "tools of change," crystals. This time presents an opportunity for crystal workers to join together in spirit to express a new Earth cycle of life.

Humanity's New Age is only a very small part of this larger Earth cycle. People are a minority of the Earth Mother's children, but our egos don't always accept that. On this planet there are more minerals, plants, insects, fish, birds, and animals than there are humans. Sensitive, caring humans are tuning into this larger family consciousness. We also like to think we are tuning and programming crystals and the Earth. It's working the other way this time as well; the Earth, the Universe, and the crystals are tuning us at the same time. This process leads to a healthy life balance for all forms and all beings on this planet. We, the people, are changing life on Earth and we are being changed by our relationship to life on Earth.

This could be described as an alchemical transformation that happens when we work with crystals and crystal tools. Building and working with these crystal tools—spiritually, mentally and physically—actually brings about growth and awareness as we work to interface with the spirit of Nature. This growth is part of and in harmony with Universal Intelligence. We are ready for the opportunity to be actively conscious of our relationship to life, as part of the Universal Being. Using crystal tools and wearing crystal ornaments in ritual or in everyday life takes on a deeper significance.

Like *Crystal Power, Crystal Spirit* can open pathways to further experimentation with new ideas. Wearing crystal anklets can connect us more deeply with the Earth energies. Wearing crystal bracelets, rings and pendants allows us to connect more closely with fellow humans. Wearing any combination of crystal jewelry can enhance the Earth's healing energy while using a crystal healing rod. A crystal crown or headband can connect us to greater spiritual realities. Using any crystal or crystal tool can help us be more aware of our kinship with all of Nature: the Earth, fish, birds, animals and the web of life that connects us all together.

Describing the spirit of crystals is much like trying to describe the experiences of seeing or sensing a rainbow. The rainbow is beauty, peace and harmony, yet it is manifested by light photons reflecting off tiny droplets of water as seen from the angle of the conscious awareness of the observer. No two observers see exactly the same rainbow from the same angle. Likewise, using words to describe a rainbow as a giant arc across the sky with bands of many colors is not even close to the experience of seeing one yourself.

The experience of the spirit of crystals is similar, since it too is barely translatable in words. The best way I've found to share the experience is to describe how to build some crystal creations using techniques that will allow us all to experience being at one with ourselves and at one with Nature and the Universe.

Crystal Spirit is composed of what crystal people have asked for, and it includes a wide variety of crystal devices and uses: many types of crystal rods and healing techniques, pyramids, computer and black box interface, culminating in the Crystal Pipe. It spans a wide spectrum of experience from the traditions of *Crystal Power* on into the future generations of the Crystal Revolution.

Introduction
Vision of the Crystal Pipe

"This is not the end of a search. It is the beginning of a New Age of knowledge, understanding and experience along the crystal path through the Universe that is us."

In the beginning of my exploration of the crystal world, there were no crystal energy rods, headbands, pyramids or any of the other crystal energy tools that are being built and used in so many countries throughout the world today.

For me, over a decade and a half ago there was only the medicine pipe and a quartz crystal. These two simple energy tools were my key for unlocking the universal doors to crystal power and so much more. Making prayers to the Great Spirit for the Earth Mother and the beings that live on her (all of them) led to the crystal technology that was later placed in the hands of researchers around the world. These regular prayers, in a circle with a quartz crystal in the center, were the key to an expanded awareness of Universal Energy, because it brought the understanding and feeling of the oneness of all things into everyday life. The pipe was offered to the six directions: the powers of the East, South, West, North, the Great Spirit and the Earth Mother. The first crystal healing rod came from the practice of making prayers with the pipe to send out healing energy from the crystal circle. The first healing rod, about eight inches long with a single-termination crystal in each end, developed from a vision of the crystal healing circle, and it is in a form that anyone could build, carry and use at any time, anywhere on the planet.

The large crystal generator-communicator developed from the crystal in the center of the circle. The pipe crystal circle allowed people to reach out with their awareness to encompass the whole Earth with healing energy. Later it allowed people to reach out with their conscious awareness through the Universe to the stars and star people. The copper cup and plate were added to the crystal at the center of the circle, as described in *Crystal Power*.

Dozens of other crystal inventions were brought into being and shared with other crystal people around the world during this 14-year cycle. The main requirements of the new tools were that they be beneficial for Earth healing and individual development while being economical and simple to build or use. The consistent factor throughout this period of invention and reinvention was the pipe ceremony during Full Moons, Equinoxes and Solstices.

During this time I had a recurring vision of a new type of pipe that would be accessible to all people during the new Earth cycle. This was the vision of the Crystal Pipe—to combine crystals and the sacred pipe of the traditional Earth-healing people into a tool that all could build and use.

At the time of the major cycle change in the summer of 1987, 14 years after I built the first crystal healing rod, the Crystal Pipe came into being. This happened at the time of the Harmonic Convergence.

The Crystal Pipe is a new tool for the beginning of a new Earth cycle. This Crystal Pipe is described at the end of this book, which is another beginning for us all. Included here are all the crystal tools that led me along the path, from the crystal rod to the crystal pipe.

Crystal Spirit describes the results of my 24-year search for definitive knowledge and understanding of self and Universe. Fourteen years of this conscious search involved the research, development, and use of quartz crystals and energy tools made from them.

1 Crystals of the Ancient Past

"There are many writings, both ancient and modern, about the secrets of the Universe. None contain all of what you seek. Only you contain all of what you seek."

THE CROSS AND THE SWORD

Thousands of years ago, at a time of wide understanding of the Universal Spirit energies, the Atlantean Crystal Cross was brought into being. The four equal arms of this crystal cross breathed as if alive with the four forces of the Universal Creator. When this life-renewing cross was placed on the Earth with its arms pointing to the North, South, East and West, the energy of the four powers of the winds flowed through it. It represented the life-giving waters of the crossed rivers that sustained the continent. Through the misuse and loss of knowledge of the Spirit, the cross had one arm replaced with a long blade, which evolved into a crystal sword. Through the decadence of civilization, the other two crystal arms disappeared, and this became the sword of magic used in the battles of divided humankind. The last one of these was called Excalibur; it is still a spirit energy device with one stone on the end of the handle. Later this became only a sword with no crystals or stones at all.

In our present time, dim memories remanifested the crystal-force knives and Excalibur swords with one crystal on the end. Even more recently, the sword with the cross of three crystal arms reappeared. Also in modern times, the blade has been replaced with the long arm of the cross and the crystal. This has emerged as the Crux Crystallum in the form symbolic of Christianity of the last 2,000 years. Despite the symbolic nature of the cross, regular swords have been used more often than the cross in the short history of Christianity. As we strive toward a new era of peace, the Crux Crystallum is once again in use. But even now, the long arm of this cross is sometimes shortened to become the equal and balanced Atlantean Crystal Cross of the four spirit forces of creation.

THE PITCHFORK OF THE GODS— TRIDENT KRYSTALLOS

The trident has been associated with Neptune and Poseidon, and with the lost island of Atlantis that sank beneath the oceans.

Amid earthquakes and volcanic eruptions of the last Atlantean battle between the forces of light and darkness, a group of white-robed warrior priests emerged from an underground installation, armed with a new type of crystal power rod, the crystal trident. With blue-white beams of energy, they sought to neutralize the destructive energy reactions of the giant domed crystal powerhouses of Atlantis. The blue-white beams of energy poured forth against the red-white flashes of energy within the domes.

The trident-armed warriors succeeded only in delaying the final destruction long enough for their brothers and sisters to flee the lost island in ships of both sea and air. All the crystal trident warriors stayed on the island and held the massive energies in check, sacrificing themselves so that their people could escape to the colonies both to the east and to the west of Atlantis. All the crystal tridents and their carriers disappeared beneath the seas.

Thousands of years later, the warrior-priests and priestesses would inhabit new bodies and once again take up the crystal tridents to neutralize the forces of negativity. That time is now!

ATLANTEAN CRYSTAL CROSS

The Atlantean Crystal Cross is one of the more compact of the new generation of crystal energy rods, measuring only about seven inches from point to point, depending on the size of the quartz crystals used. It is a very powerful archetype from the most ancient of Earth's history.

In Atlantis it represented the cross of the four rivers that divided the main continent. This cross is a balanced crystal device radiating healing Earth energy. With a circle around it, it becomes the symbol of Earth. It is the Hopi sign for land and good life when four smaller circles are centered in the four sections of the cross and circle. It combines the energy of the Universe with the energy of the Earth Mother. This crystal rein-vention is alive at all times as soon as it is constructed. Crystal power/healing rods are active when held by a person, and passive (but still radiating energy) even when they are laid down. This crystal cross is active at high intensity energy levels at all times. This healing/balancing energy increases when the cross is used in the center of a healing or meditation circle. It is cleared by touching the crystals and projecting the white light through them. In a circle of crystal light workers, it can be used by itself or with a large generator crystal for expanding the circle or sphere of white-light healing energy to encompass the whole planet.

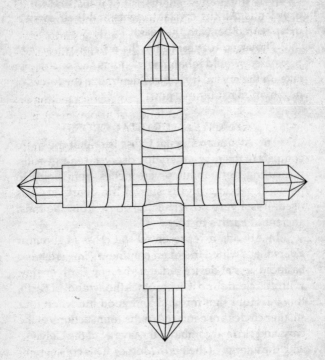

Atlantean Crystal Cross

In most cases the energy is not visualized for a specific healing use. This is a decision that is usually left up to the conscious being we know as Earth. She knows the best way to use energy for balance and healing. Our work is often to bring in more energy from the rest of creation for her to use and disperse. As with the other crystal tools, projecting a feeling of universal love and the emotion of at-one-ment is a good basis of operation.

During this time the individual operator or guide for the group should consciously realize that he or she is an expression of the Creator. (Not just connected to the Creator, but expressing and projecting as the source of Universal Energy.) This is an experience that expresses the energy flow better if it is happy and joyful, not serious and tense. Spontaneous toning or chanting can add a lot to a crystal circle when you are using the Atlantean Crystal Cross.

Construction

The Atlantean Crystal Cross is sometimes known as the Earth Cross. Its equal arms are about seven inches from crystal tip to tip, depending on the length of the crystals used. The center frame is a ½-inch diameter copper tee with a ⅜-inch hole drilled in the top. A ½-inch copper coupling is cut or notched to fit the tee so that an equal cross is formed. The coupling is then soldered securely to the tee. The soldered area can be sanded or filed to create a neater, more uniform surface. The arms of the cross are formed by mounting a ¼-inch to ½-inch diameter quartz crystal into a ½-inch copper coupling. If the crystal diameter is smaller than the coupling, leather, copper mesh, or copper shims are fitted and glued around the crystal inside the coupling for a secure fit.

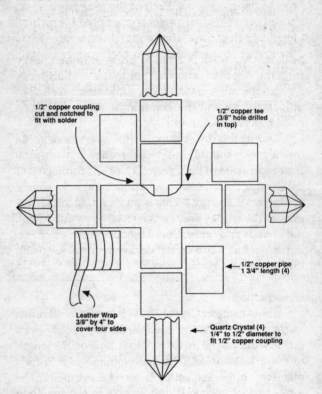

1/2" copper coupling
cut and notched to
fit with solder

1/2" copper tee
(3/8" hole drilled
in top)

1/2" copper pipe
1 3/4" length (4)

Leather Wrap
3/8" by 4" to
cover four sides

Quartz Crystal (4)
1/4" to 1/2" diameter to
fit 1/2" copper coupling

Atlantean Crystal Cross
Construction

Four crystals need to be mounted this way for the tips of the cross arms. Each of the four arms is composed of a ½-inch diameter copper pipe 1¾ inches in length. Each of these arms is glued as it is fitted inside the center copper cross, then each copper coupling with crystal is glued and fitted at the end of the cross arm. This leaves about an inch of each arm between the coupling and the center cross that can be wrapped with a ⅜-inch wide strip of leather, or other material of any color you prefer.

Like the other crystal rod models, length and diameter can be increased or decreased according to what you feel is right for you. These prototypes serve as a guide for further creation and modifications to serve the energy of the individual light being. Since each quartz crystal is a unique individual and each light worker is also unique, one size certainly does not fit all! The perception of the relationships of energy fields is in a constant state of change and expression, so our creations reflect this moving balance of harmony. These are creations that are alive with the universal creative energy. Follow your own feelings and intuition for modifications or additions. Your inner self knows better than anyone else what is best for *you*.

This crystal tool works with the Universal Energy of the Earth Mother. This nurturing, healing energy supports the life force of all the beings of the planet. The cross channels this force for balance in plants, animals and people.

Some crystal healers use the cross in the right hand while using a flowing motion of turning, whirling and spiraling the energy around or through the energy field of the being they are balancing and harmonizing. Others prefer the same motions with the cross in the left hand, visualizing the radiation of light energy. Some crystal workers say that the right hand is for transmitting and the left hand is for receiving energy when using crystal tools. Like many other dogmatic statements and set rules, there are always exceptions. There are people who do great crystal energy work using the left hand for transmitting and the right hand for receiving energy. This may have to do with a person being right- or left-handed or right- or left-brained.

There is another alternative. Some people are using two crystal crosses, one in each hand. It appears that these balance and complement each other, with one transmitting and one receiving, as well as both transmitting at the same time or both receiving at the same time. This seems to be showing us again that we are the key energy connection. We are also learning about the importance of polarity and balancing the positive/negative, male/female energy within ourselves as the Universal Energy flows through us. You are the best judge of what feels right and works for you. Experiment and determine your way; whether it is the same as others or not, it's right for you.

CRUX CRYSTALLUM

The Crux Crystallum is an Atlantean form that is familiar to many people as a powerful religious symbol and archetype. This is a form that utilizes the four forces or directions of the Earth. As an individual crystal energy rod held in your hand, the cross radiates a strong pattern of universal light for healing and balance. For groups or circles of light workers, this crystal cross can be placed upright in the Earth for manifesting the spiritual and material projection of energy. Standing on the Earth, the top three quartz crystals of the trinity

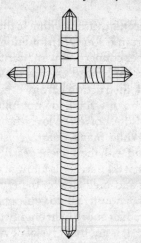

Crux Crystallum

emit energy for human spiritual development. This Pleiades crystal tool is a standard for personal growth, balance, self-healing and attunement to the universal creative force. It is an excellent form for radiating the most powerful force in the Universe, *love*. Feeling the spirit of the heart of love while visualizing the white-light energy is one of the best uses for this crystal healing tool. There is a great feeling of being at one with the Creator/Christ Consciousness involved with this crystal cross. It radiates the crystal energy of our highest ideals and reminds us of our true inner self.

The individual experiences with this crystal power tool are many, according to the perceptions and feelings of the person using it. What *you* do with the crystal cross is dependent on not only your understanding but also your feeling of the patterns and the relationships of constantly moving fields of universal creative energy. It all begins with self-healing, balance and love, radiating energy from within to the energy fields of all beings around you. Deep intuition and guidance from your inner connection with Spirit are the determining factors for how to use this tool.

Outward instructions from others in words, whether spoken or written, do not fully describe the experience of the power of love through the Crux Crystallum. While many quartz crystal tools have been associated with the ancient past or the far future, the reality is that they are tools for right now. It may be wise to think and meditate on the crystal cross and what it means or how it feels to you, personally, before you use it to radiate more light energy than it radiates of itself at first. It is another crystal device that is alive and active as soon as it is built.

There are several ways to use this crystal tool. The obvious way is by holding the long arm at the bottom in your hand while visualizing and feeling a white or golden energy field of love, peace, trust and well-being radiating outward as a growing sphere of life energy.

The cross also can be held with the center in the palm of your hand, like the Atlantean Cross, with the long arm parallel to your forearm. A field of energy can be radiated or a beam of healing energy visualized as emitting from the shorter arm on top of the cross. This position can be reversed with the long arm pointed outward for use as a healing rod.

Another position that can be used is to hold the shorter top arm in your hand like a sword grip, with the energy beam emitting through the crystal at the end of the long arm.

It is probably more than coincidence that a reversed or upside-down cross becomes a sword. There is a lesson in both symbolism and polarity here that can be explored by personal meditation. This could show many different things to individuals, depending on the person's experiences and awareness. The Crux Crystallum may prove to be a self-healing, self-teaching tool at its finest.

Construction

The Crux Crystallum is also constructed around a center copper cross. This is formed from a ½-inch copper tee with a ⅜-inch hole drilled in the center top. A ½-inch diameter copper coupling is drilled or notched to fit the top, forming the center cross. These two pieces are then soldered squarely and securely to make a strong central unit. This is another version of the Atlantean cross that requires four quartz crystals—from ¼-inch in diameter up to ½-inch in diameter with an approximate length of one inch. The four crystals are mounted and glued into the ½-inch copper couplings using leather, copper mesh, or copper shims for a secure fit. The top three cross pieces are ½-inch diameter copper pipe cut to two-inch lengths. These are fitted into the center cross and glued securely. The bottom cross handgrip is a seven-inch length of ½-inch copper pipe fitted and glued into the bottom of the tee/cross. The four crystals in their coupling mounts are then attached to the ends of the four cross arms with glue. It is a good idea to pre-fit these first without the instant bonding glue to see that they slide on easily with a slight twist. If they don't, it may be necessary to file or sand the edges of the copper pipe. The same fitting procedure should be used for all connections, since the instant bonding glue seldom gives you a second chance at fitting the connections.

After the main unit is assembled, the half-inch diameter pipe sections are then wrapped with strips

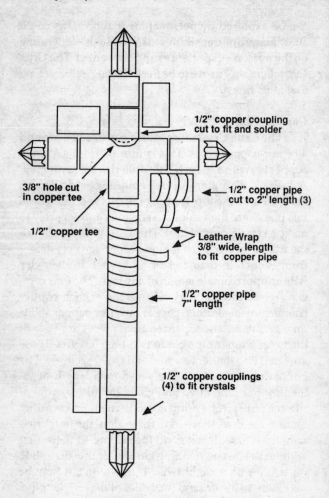

1/2" copper coupling
cut to fit and solder

**3/8" hole cut
in copper tee**

1/2" copper tee

**1/2" copper pipe
cut to 2" length (3)**

**Leather Wrap
3/8" wide, length
to fit copper pipe**

**1/2" copper pipe
7" length**

**1/2" copper couplings
(4) to fit crystals**

Crux Crystallum
Construction

of leather glued in place or with another covering material using your choice of color. This is another very powerful "live" unit with the energy of the Creator, Lord of the Universe. This is a projector and radiator of the loving power of the Christ Consciousness in action. It is also an exciting and awesome thought/ feeling amplifier. This device and a light-being operator express the kind of loving energy that the Earth is much in need of at this time. Again, please use your own judgment and intuition in building or using this. It is quite a learning experience tool, as you'll discover for yourself.

TRIDENT KRYSTALLOS

The trident is held like an ordinary crystal power rod. It can be visualized as radiating a field of Universal Energy or projecting three parallel beams of blue-white light energy, or perceived as three beams merging into a wide beam from an energy cone emission point.

The energy from crystal tools can be visualized with spirals and waves within the moving pattern of a field radiation or beam projection. The Trident Krystallos, like the other crystal tools, shows us much about ourselves: our attitudes, perceptions and awareness.

At first glance the Trident Krystallos is one of the least familiar quartz crystal tools of our time. The trident is associated with the traditions of Neptune and Poseidon, and with the sea and the sea gods. The Crystal Trident today is more likely to be related to the seas of Universal Energy. This device is most often used to project beams of white-light energy, in contrast to the field radiations of the crystal crosses. The trident does indeed start radiating a field of energy as

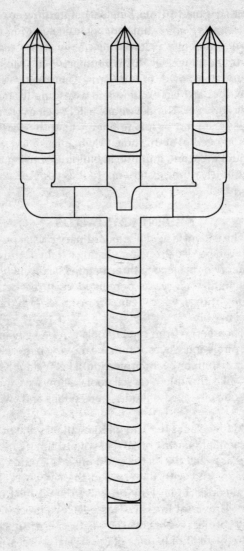

Trident Krystallos

soon as it is constructed, but its most startling application is as an energy beam and ray projector. Most people see it as another form of the crystal power rod for disarming or neutralizing weapons and war machines of modern times. This activity is necessary to bring about the healing peace and balance of the planet Earth. Again, the motivating force is the power of love and light. Its appeal is to people who understand the nature of the healer as warrior or the warrior as healer. It reaffirms the truth of the saying, "Only the most powerful of people have the strength to be gentle."

The expression of the quartz crystal trinity is a very strong energy for our world. As with the other crystal tools, the ultimate guidance for use and responsibility comes from the inner self as creator. The crystal trident is another archetype of the Earth philosophies expressed by strong, spiritual light energy manifestation. This tool is sometimes surprising, but with an important kinship for many people of our time. The trident is one of the tools we are just now starting to learn about and explore with and within ourselves.

Interestingly enough, with its high intensity energy pattern and dramatic appearance, it can still be used as a tool for healing and balance in the way that we use crystal healing rods. The color of the covering can be chosen for your rod, with your feeling for balance and harmony expressed as you like it. This type of tool tends to widen the definition of healing more than is usually perceived. While it can be set in the Earth for a circle, this is very rarely done. It is generally used as an individual, hand-held crystal energy device. As with the others, there is no better authority than your own judgment.

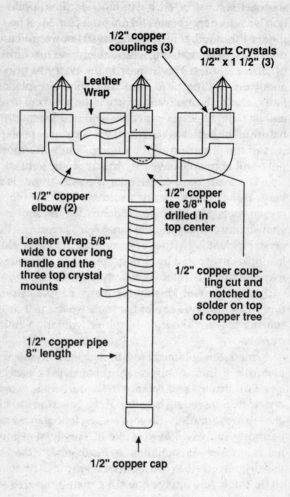

1/2" copper couplings (3)

Leather Wrap

Quartz Crystals 1/2" x 1 1/2" (3)

1/2" copper elbow (2)

1/2" copper tee 3/8" hole drilled in top center

Leather Wrap 5/8" wide to cover long handle and the three top crystal mounts

1/2" copper coupling cut and notched to solder on top of copper tree

1/2" copper pipe 8" length →

1/2" copper cap

Trident Krystallos
Construction

Construction

The Trident Krystallos is constructed around the copper tee/cross center, like the other Atlantean crosses. The ½-inch copper tee is drilled in the center top with a ⅜-inch hole, and a ½-inch coupling is drilled and notched to fit the top. The only part requiring solder for a solid connection is this tee and the coupling of the main center unit. As with the others, it may require filing or sanding at the soldered connection. All the other connections are secured with instant bonding glue. Three quartz crystals are needed for this construction. The sizes can be up to ½ inch in diameter and up to 1½ inches in length as an approximate guide for this model. The crystals are mounted in the three ½-inch diameter copper couplings, using leather, copper mesh, or copper shims glued into place. These can then be set aside to dry while the main unit is assembled. An eight-inch length of ½-inch diameter copper pipe is glued into the bottom opening of the center cross as the handgrip arm. A ½-inch copper cap is then glued on the end of this long section. The two side arms are formed by inserting ½-inch copper elbows into the side openings of the center cross. These should be fitted, like the other parts, first without glue. When they are glued in, they should be lined up vertically with the center top opening of the cross. The three top arms are two-inch lengths of ½-inch copper pipe glued into the three top openings. The three couplings with the crystals already mounted are glued to the three uprights. The crystal trident is then ready for the final leather wrap or covering with the material of your choice. The color of the covering should be chosen according to what you feel comfortable with. The Trident Crystallos, especially when covered in black leather, is startling and disarming, literally. This tool is quite frequently used to heal and balance by sending white-light energy to disarm weapons of war, which indicate disease on the Earth. It is another quartz crystal device that is alive with energy as soon as it is assembled.

2 Crystal Rods of Light—
The Healing Rods

"We're seeing and feeling the Spirit within our manifested physical world. Perhaps next, we'll experience the Spirit of the Spirit."

There are many new crystal rods and other devices being invented or reinvented around the world every day by people like you and I. Many modifications have been used, and they all seem to work. In wrapping the rods, leather, yarn, cloth, plastic tape, shrink tubing, etc., have been used with equal success. The length and diameter of the rods has varied from pencil size to seven-foot long models. These have been made using tiny crystals as well as very large ones.

Again, each size and model has proved adequate. All types of quartz crystals have been used: clear, cloudy, smoky and amethyst, in all shapes, sizes and conditions. They all worked for the purpose of the people who built them. The key has always been the spirit, the consciousness of the light beings, the co-creators themselves. The present era of spiritual expression is working wonders in our world each and every day.

Healing rods can be large, medium or small, but they all work the same way. A beam of energy made up of subatomic particles, usually outside the visible range of the human eye's spectrum, (sometimes, but not always, seen as a blue-white beam) is projected from the point of the crystal at the outer end of the rod.

This beam of energy is visualized and thought of first by the operator-healer. Energy follows thought, so the subatomic particles of Universal Energy begin instantly moving in place of the visualized beam (a fraction of a second). At the same time, the crystal at the inner end of the healing rod, pointed towards the operator-healer, is emitting a field energy that radiates toward and merges with the healer's aura or bioelectromagnetic field.

As the flow of energy is started, the healer may wish to outline a circle of energy around the subject with the outward crystal point of the rod. This is usually done from one to three times (but sometimes up to 12 times), starting at the top of the subject's head and moving in a clockwise circle. At the same time, the healer begins to feel and radiate a feeling of unconditional love and oneness with the subject. This emotional feeling by the healer determines the degree, force or amplification of the energy flowing from the crystal healing rod.

If the healer is right handed, the crystal rod is held in the right hand. If left handed, it's held in the left. The reverse is more comfortable for some people, though. Usually starting at the top of the subject's head, the healer slowly brings the rod downwards to about six inches from the body. The healer's hand without the rod follows the motion of the rod, about six inches from both the rod and the subject's body. This is so that the flow of energy can be felt. This movement is used, downward to neck and shoulders, along the arms to the hands and back up to the neck.

This motion is continued down the length of the

body and legs, then back up the body. All this time, usually five to fifteen minutes, the healer's open hand is feeling the flow of energy. At certain areas the healer will feel warm or hot spots. This usually indicates a blockage of energy in the subject—an injury or disease. The healer then directs the beam of energy from the rod to the hot spot. After a few minutes the hot spot usually turns cool, indicating that enough energy has been channeled into the area. If the area is a serious injury in the process of healing itself, it may not change from hot to cool.

After energy blockages have been dealt with and balanced in the body, the healer then returns with rod and open hand to the subject's head areas. If there were warm areas of the body, there will usually be warm areas of the head. The subject's mind, thoughts and feelings in the head area have usually reflected or expressed themselves in areas of the body, so reenergizing and balancing of the head area is necessary as the source of the affected areas is traced.

The hot spots or energy blockages are usually the symptoms. The cause can usually be traced back to the head area: mind, thoughts or even spirit. The other area that the cause can be traced to is the heart area, in which case the cause is related to negative emotions and the inability to express love for others, meaning an inability to accept and love one's self with respect.

If the energy flow does not feel strong enough at first, there is one thing a healer can do before picking up the rod. Often, this is a good standard practice to start with in any case. Visualize a baseball-sized sun or sphere of energy in front of you. Using cupped hands, form and shape this ball of energy while feeling it grow stronger in pressure. This method of starting the energy flow through the hands can augment the flow through the energy rod and crystal.

After the energy balancing of the subject is completed, it is sometimes necessary to return the flow of energy from the healer's hands to a normal flow or balance. There are two commonly used, simple techniques. One is to clench the fists tightly and release them simultaneously. The other is to relax the hands and wrists while shaking them rapidly a few times to release the excess energy flow.

The practices and techniques described here are intended to be suggestions and guidelines only. Many people develop and modify these procedures through personal experience.

The following are variations on the basic healing rod. You may, in your turn, be guided to invent other variations on these.

MINIATURE HEALING ROD

One of the most popular new styles of crystal rod is the miniature version. The reason for this is that many people now carry their crystal rods at all times, so there was a need for a size that would fit in a coat pocket or a purse. This smaller model fills the need. It can be constructed using the traditional method of splitting the copper tube to fit the crystal and covering it with leather wrap. The new method of mounting crystals uses a one-half inch wide strip of copper mesh as a shim to wrap the crystal so that it fits inside a copper coupler, which is then fitted to the copper pipe using an instant bonding glue. The total length of this rod is approximately six inches. The other difference in construction is the leather wrap. The copper pipe is wrapped in a spiral, as in the traditional method, but the leather covers just the central pipe and not the copper couplers on the ends. These are left exposed.

Miniature Healing Rod

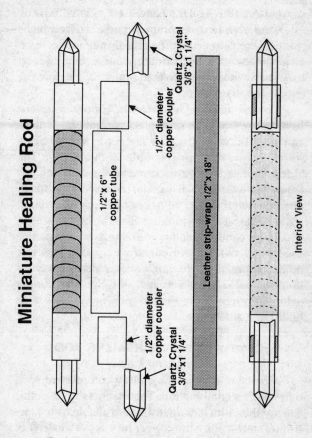

Quartz Crystal
3/8"x1 1/4"

1/2" diameter
copper coupler

1/2"x 6"
copper tube

Leather strip-wrap 1/2"x 18"

1/2" diameter
copper coupler

Quartz Crystal
3/8"x1 1/4"

Interior View

These small rods can be shortened to four or five inches, if desired, for convenience.

MAGNETIC (LODESTONE) HEALING ROD

This model in the pocket or purse size combines the healing properties of natural magnetism with quartz crystals. Natural lodestone, available from most rock shops, is loaded into the copper pipe before the crystals are mounted.

The crystals are mounted in copper couplers, using copper mesh or small pieces of leather as shims, and attached with glue. The leather is wrapped in a spiral, leaving the copper coupler ends exposed. The lodestone needs to be shaken down and sometimes tamped in with a pencil in order to pack it as tightly as possible. Even then, I've never built one that didn't rattle a little bit after assembly. Size can be changed to what feels comfortable for you. The drawings can be used as a guideline for construction. If changes or modifications occur to you, you should follow your intuition as to what you feel is right. The copper diameter can be either ½ or ¾ inch. Some have been built both smaller and larger in diameter.

CRYSTAL MAGNET HEALING ROD
(Standard Size)

Crystal and magnetic energy compliment each other in this combination. The magnets used in this rod are the ½-inch diameter size available from electronics stores. Since the copper pipe is ¾ inch, leather or copper mesh needs to be wrapped around the magnets to hold them stable inside the rod. The standard size 12-inch rod takes about 60 of these magnets. The new style rod shown with the exposed copper couplers may require a few more to touch the crystals

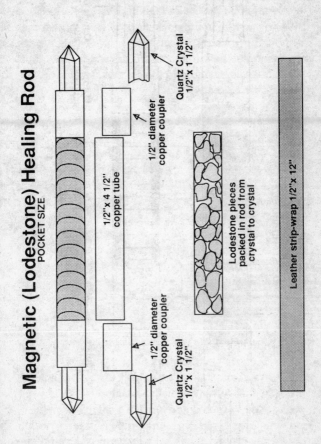

Magnetic (Lodestone) Healing Rod
POCKET SIZE

Quartz Crystal
1/2" x 1 1/2"

1/2" diameter copper coupler

1/2" x 4 1/2" copper tube

Lodestone pieces packed in rod from crystal to crystal

1/2" diameter copper coupler

Quartz Crystal
1/2" x 1 1/2"

Leather strip-wrap 1/2" x 12"

Quartz Crystal Magnet Healing Rod

STANDARD SIZE

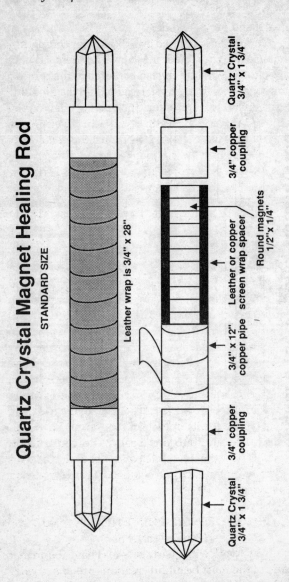

Leather wrap is 3/4" x 28"

Quartz Crystal
3/4" x 1 3/4"

3/4" copper
coupling

Round magnets
1/2" x 1/4"

Leather or copper
screen wrap spacer

3/4" x 12"
copper pipe

3/4" copper
coupling

Quartz Crystal
3/4" x 1 3/4"

at each end for a solid fit.

The crystals are fitted into the copper couplers by gluing leather or copper mesh around them as shims for a tight fit, with the crystals centered in the coupler. One coupler with the crystal is glued on the pipe, and the magnets are fitted before the other crystal coupler is glued in place. The leather wrap can cover the rod and couplers up to the crystals or just the center copper pipe, leaving the couplers exposed. The crystals tend to focus and project the magnetic field with the visualization of the white-light beam amplified by the emotional healing power of love. This operates in the same manner as the other power healing rods.

TWIN CRYSTAL HEALING ROD

This rod follows the same pattern as the smaller rods and can run up to 8½ inches in length, depending on the length of crystals used. Twin termination quartz crystals are used. These are just the natural growth of two crystals side by side with the points in the same direction. One-half inch diameter by one inch length is adequate, although any size will work. The most interesting aspect of this rod is that because of the two points on each crystal, twin beams of white-light energy projecting from each end of the rod must be visualized for its operation. These can be visualized as blending into one beam. The construction shown is with the new style copper couplers used as crystal mounts at each end of the rod. Leather covering is also used.

CRYSTAL PENCIL-POINT HEALING ROD
(Purse or Pocket Size)

In my work with quartz crystals I have found that many of the most beautiful creations are of a smaller

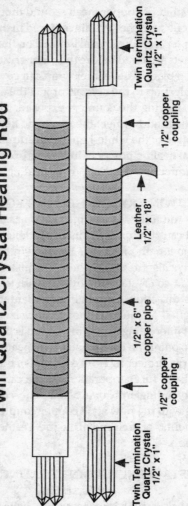

Twin Quartz Crystal Healing Rod

Twin Termination Quartz Crystal 1/2" x 1"

1/2" copper coupling

Leather 1/2" x 18"

1/2" x 6" copper pipe

1/2" copper coupling

Twin Termination Quartz Crystal 1/2" x 1"

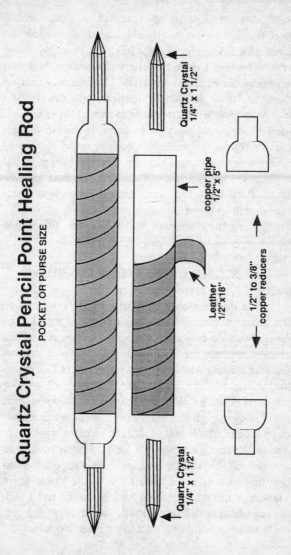

Quartz Crystal Pencil Point Healing Rod

POCKET OR PURSE SIZE

Quartz Crystal
1/4" x 1 1/2"

copper pipe
1/2" x 5"

Leather
1/2" x 18"

1/2" to 3/8"
copper reducers

Quartz Crystal
1/4" x 1 1/2"

size. Some of these are so clear and perfectly formed that they can't be overlooked as a source of the Universal Energy on Earth. In order to enjoy these crystal beings, I designed a special healing rod that accommodates these crystals. Quite a number of these are only ¼ inch in diameter and one to two inches in length. It is possible to mount these in a ½-inch diameter copper pipe by using ½-inch to ⅜-inch copper reducers. Leather or copper mesh is used to wrap the crystals, and glue for attaching them to the reducers. This is a unique design. The smaller size crystals still have the same natural subatomic structure that links them to the universal matrix of creative energy, so they operate just as well as the larger sizes.

MODIFIED CRYSTAL HEALING ROD
(Large Pencil Point Style)

This design was so pleasing in the smaller size that it was used as a model for a larger size rod. This requires more copper fittings of various sizes. The smaller crystals are still used, with the rod size reduced from the standard ¾ inch to ½ inch. The drawing shows the crystals mounted in ½-inch copper couplers. Each of these is fitted to a ¾- to ½-inch reducer by using a one-inch length of ½-inch diameter copper pipe. The larger end of the reducer is joined to a ¾-inch copper coupling, which is then attached to the ¾-inch midsection and leather wrapped. Instant bonding glue is used for all the connections. For a pleasing contrast, any color leather can be used with the copper ends left uncovered. This style, with a partial leather covering, is becoming quite popular.

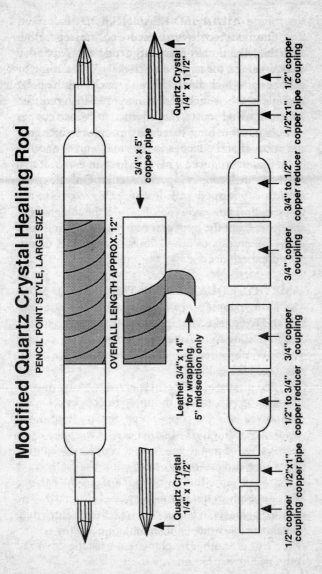

Modified Quartz Crystal Healing Rod
PENCIL POINT STYLE, LARGE SIZE

Quartz Crystal
1/4" x 1 1/2"

3/4" x 5" copper pipe

OVERALL LENGTH APPROX. 12"

Leather 3/4"x 14" for wrapping 5" midsection only

Quartz Crystal 1/4" x 1 1/2"

1/2" copper coupling copper pipe

1/2" to 3/4" copper reducer

3/4" copper coupling

3/4" copper coupling

3/4" to 1/2" copper reducer

1/2"x1" copper pipe coupling

1/2" copper coupling

MODIFIED HEALING ROD

The modified design was carried one step further with the reduction from the large rod being expanded back up to use the larger size crystals. This is done by mounting ¾-inch diameter by 1½-inch length quartz crystals in the ¾-inch end of a ¾- to ½-inch reducer. As the drawing shows, this is joined to ½-inch copper pipe, two inches long, that runs through a ½-inch copper coupler and attaches to the small end of another ¾- to ½-inch reducer. This provides an end unit that fits the ¾-inch copper pipe midsection. Only this midsection is wrapped with leather. This is one of the more radical new style rods. It works the same way as the others, but the appearance is likely to bring back many memories of other times—of Atlantis or off-world experiences.

AMETHYST QUARTZ CRYSTAL HEALING ROD

Many people feel a kinship with amethyst crystals and have asked if they could be used with quartz and in healing rods. Amethyst and quartz crystals are a good combination for healing rods, as shown in this standard-size model.

The quartz and amethyst crystals, ¾ by one- to two-inch length, can be mounted in copper couplers (as shown) or in the copper pipe directly (traditional style). Accordingly, the leather can be wrapped up to the crystals, or just to the copper couplers, whatever you desire and feel comfortable with. The violet color vibration of amethyst provides a peaceful balance with the high frequency energy of clear quartz. The balance helps us to feel at one with the creator while visualizing the white-light energy for a healthy energy field. This is another machine that uses the power of universal love as an energy force.

Modified Healing Rod

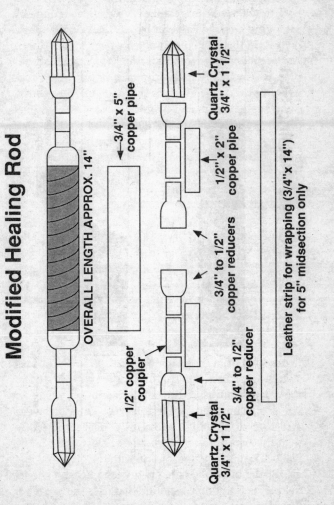

OVERALL LENGTH APPROX. 14"

3/4" x 5" copper pipe

Quartz Crystal 3/4" x 1 1/2"

1/2" x 2" copper pipe

3/4" to 1/2" copper reducers

Leather strip for wrapping (3/4"x 14") for 5" midsection only

1/2" copper coupler

3/4" to 1/2" copper reducer

Quartz Crystal 3/4" x 1 1/2"

Amethyst Quartz Crystal Healing Rod

LARGE SIZE

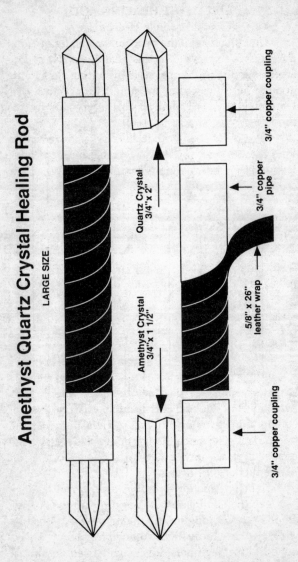

Quartz Crystal
3/4" x 2"

Amethyst Crystal
3/4" x 1 1/2"

3/4" copper coupling

3/4" copper pipe

5/8" x 26"
leather wrap

3/4" copper coupling

AMETHYST HEALING ROD
(Traditional Style-Medium Size)

The full effect of the peaceful balancing of violet amethyst is expressed in this healing rod. It is constructed in the traditional style by cutting slots in the copper pipe for fitting the amethyst crystals. The leather is also wrapped up to the crystals in this model.

The size is smaller than the standard and larger than the pocket or purse size. It uses an eight-inch length of ½-inch diameter copper tubing. When the crystals are fitted, the overall length is approximately 9½ inches. The color of the amethyst crystals ranges from a light violet to a deep purple. Instant bonding glue is used to attach the crystals and the leather wrap. This rod represents spiritual healing for the light beings that we are. The emanation of peaceful vibrations makes this rod a favorite of many people who work with crystals.

SMOKY QUARTZ/CLEAR QUARTZ HEALING ROD
(Traditional Style Using Extra Large Crystals)

At just over 12 inches in length, this rod shows a striking contrast—a clear quartz crystal one inch by two inches in one end and a smoky quartz crystal of equal size in the other end. This rod is fashioned in the traditional style, since the larger crystals require the copper pipe (¾-inch by 10-inch) to be slotted and flared outward for fitting.

This combination provides a powerful balance between the elimination of the more subtle negative emotions and thoughts and the inflowing of positive white light in a more highly refined frequency. This is not a rod for beginners. It is usually used with great

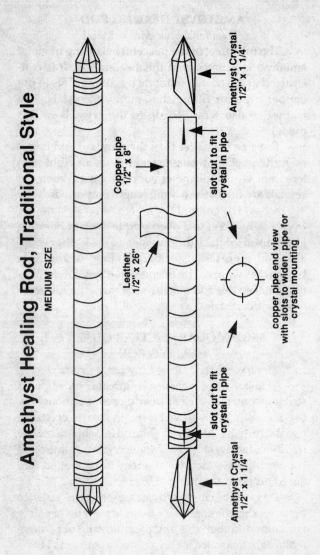

Amethyst Healing Rod, Traditional Style
MEDIUM SIZE

Amethyst Crystal
1/2" x 1 1/4"

Copper pipe
1/2" x 8"

slot cut to fit
crystal in pipe

Leather
1/2" x 26"

copper pipe end view
with slots to widen pipe for
crystal mounting

slot cut to fit
crystal in pipe

Amethyst Crystal
1/2" x 1 1/4"

Smokey Quartz/Clear Quartz Healing Rod

TRADITIONAL STYLE USING LARGE CRYSTALS

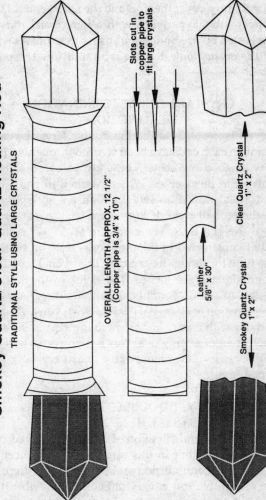

OVERALL LENGTH APPROX. 12 1/2"
(Copper pipe is 3/4" x 10")

Slots cut in copper pipe to fit large crystals

Leather
5/8" x 30"

Clear Quartz Crystal
1" x 2"

Smokey Quartz Crystal
1" x 2"

care in very special instances. The leather is wrapped up to and around the crystals in the traditional style, since it must cover the slots and the flared ends of the copper tube. Experience with other crystal rods is suggested before building or using this rod. As with all the crystal tools, the use is an individual responsibility.

CRYSTAL DOUBLE TERMINATION HEALING ROD

This one really is a double double. Crystals with a point on each end have been favored throughout history as good medicine. These are balanced energy entities in themselves. When matched in pairs in a rod, they project an intense high energy spiritual healing for all areas of consciousness.

This rod is the standard size (¾" x 12" copper pipe) constructed in the traditional style by slotting the tube for fitting the crystals. The overall length is approximately 14 inches. The color of the leather wrap depends on your personal preference. As in the construction of all crystal devices, what you feel comfortable with is very important to the expression and projection of energy use. This is a powerful healing rod because of the nature of the quartz crystals combined in it.

AMETHYST DOUBLE TERMINATION CRYSTAL HEALING ROD

The peaceful vibration of violet is amplified and intensified further in this rod. "Intensely peaceful" seems like a contradiction of terms, but the feeling one gets from this rod is very difficult to describe. It is closer to pocket or purse size, since most people like to carry it often.

Quartz Crystal Double Termination Healing Rod

Double termination
Quartz Crystal
7/8" x 1 3/4"

Copper pipe
3/4" x 12"

Slots to widen
pipe to fit
crystals

Leather wrap
1/2" x 24"
(can be several
shorter lengths)

Double termination
Quartz Crystal
7/8" x 1 3/4"

Amethyst Double Termination Crystal Healing Rod

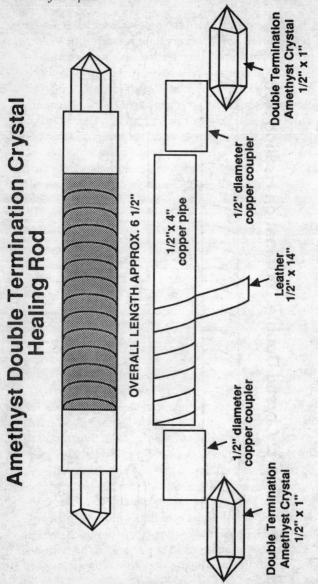

OVERALL LENGTH APPROX. 6 1/2"

Double Termination Amethyst Crystal 1/2" x 1"

1/2" diameter copper coupler

1/2" x 4" copper pipe

Leather 1/2" x 14"

1/2" diameter copper coupler

Double Termination Amethyst Crystal 1/2" x 1"

It is constructed in the new style with the double termination amethyst crystals mounted in ½-inch copper couplers using leather or copper mesh as shims. The leather wrap covers the central handgrip part of the rod with the copper coupler ends left uncovered. The contrast is pleasing with almost any color of leather you might choose. The shade of amethyst can be light or dark, according to what you like the best. This is a very comfortable personal healing rod. This combination has a calming effect with a wide energy field around it. It sometimes takes awhile to find the double termination amethyst crystals, but it is usually well worth it when you do.

OPEN-END HEALING ROD WITH
DOUBLE TERMINATION CRYSTAL

This is one of the most innovative models in use. It has one double termination quartz crystal in one end and is built in the larger size, but it is anything but standard. At the crystal end the leather is wrapped all the way to the crystal in the traditional style. At the other end a copper coupler is attached and left exposed as well as open. The leather is wrapped up to the coupler, as it is in the new style rods.

It is a very special tool, with the energy consciousness focused on the one crystal. The full potential of this rod has not been expressed yet, but future experiments will help us understand it and ourselves at the same rate of unfoldment. This is a bit different, even for a crystal energy rod. The difference is in the copper chamber. Most are capped or sealed by another crystal to form a closed chamber. In this model, the double termination crystal takes the place of a single termination crystal in each end. The open end of the chamber may make the channeling flows of energy stronger.

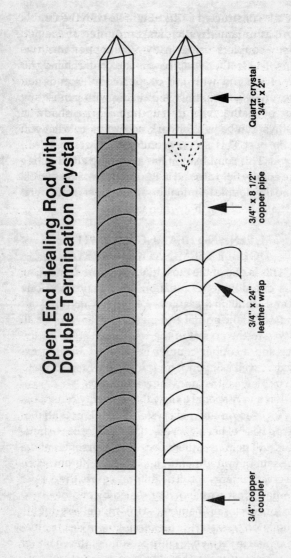

Open End Healing Rod with Double Termination Crystal

Quartz crystal
3/4" x 2"

3/4" x 8 1/2"
copper pipe

3/4" x 24"
leather wrap

3/4" copper coupler

CRYSTAL PALM SIZE SELF-HEALING ROD

This rod is radically different in size, shape and use from any other. The rod is slightly less than five inches in length and uses the standard ¾-inch diameter copper pipe. It uses one single termination quartz crystal and one double termination quartz crystal mounted in the 2½-inch length of copper pipe. The leather wrap extends up to the ends of the tube to each crystal. It is constructed in the traditional style, but without slotting the copper pipe ends. The crystals are chosen to fit the ¾-inch tube diameter. Sometimes flat-sided quartz crystals, which have been referred to as knowledge crystals, are used. Knowledge is healing. This is especially true in the case of self-healing, which is the purpose of this energy rod.

While any healing rod can be used for self-healing, this rod has been manifested specifically for balancing the light-being you call yourself. It is provided for individuals who wish to increase their spiritual expression of light and truth to a much higher degree, in order to manifest the spiritual through the physical world.

The difference in use is that the thumb of the hand holding the rod is placed on the side of the double termination crystal. This begins with a period of at-one-ment with the energy of the Creator to the highest degree that you know how. The visualization is of your aura being very bright with a blue-white or golden light, and it is augmented and amplified by the energy radiating in a field from the rod. With this healing rod, a beam is very seldom used, because the energy field is of primary importance for strengthening and balancing. This is definitely for serious self-development. Your intuition and your inner self are your guides for individual operation of this crystal

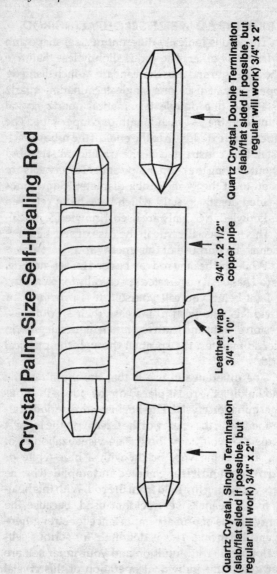

Crystal Palm-Size Self-Healing Rod

Quartz Crystal, Double Termination (slab/flat sided if possible, but regular will work) 3/4" x 2"

3/4" x 2 1/2" copper pipe

Leather wrap 3/4" x 10"

Quartz Crystal, Single Termination (slab/flat sided if possible, but regular will work) 3/4" x 2"

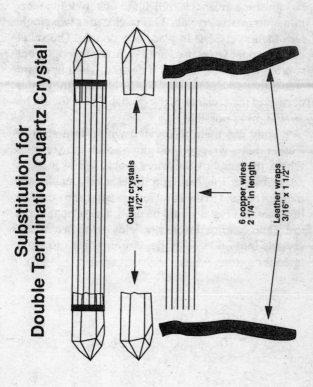

Substitution for Double Termination Quartz Crystal

Quartz crystals 1/2" x 1"

6 copper wires 2 1/4" in length

Leather wraps 3/16" x 1 1/2"

implement. Instruction outside yourself is of little help in this area. You are the ultimate authority.

SUBSTITUTION FOR DOUBLE TERMINATION QUARTZ CRYSTAL

In some areas it is difficult to obtain double termination quartz crystals. This device uses two single termination crystals in place of a double. The small gauge copper wires used are 2¼ inches in length, but shorter wires can be used if desired. The important step is that each of the six wires be glued to the center of each of the six sides of the crystal. These should be as straight as possible.

They can then be covered with a thin strip of leather that is wrapped and glued around the crystals where the ends of the wires touch. While it looks rather fragile, this really produces a very stable unit that can be held in the hand for use where any double termination crystal would be used. The copper wires unify and balance the energy fields of the two quartz crystals into one energy field, tuning them to work together as one.

3 Crystal Rods of Light— The Power Rods

"All people are knowledgeable—some more, some less—in the many possible areas of life."

TECHNIQUES FOR POWER ROD USE

Wherever there is a crystal, there can be an energy balancing or healing effect. This being the case, a power rod with a crystal in one end (either double or single termination) and a cap on the other end can be used as a healing rod by using the healing rod techniques.

The power rod can also be used in other ways to project energy outward from the operator to any area of the world. I believe this more widely broadens the definition of healing than what we have usually thought. From that perspective, it's all energy balancing or healing. On the other hand, while healing rods were specifically constructed to be intimately connected to the energy field of the operator, power rods were not. Because of the nature of crystals and humans, power rods are connected to the operator in a different way, but greater or lesser degrees of connection may not be the proper term to apply here.

The power rod's crystal energy action has a lot to do with the intention that goes into its construction. The intent of both power rod and operator is to channel or project a large flow of Universal Energy in an intense beam of blue-white light energy (sometimes visible but usually not) over longer distances than one would think of in relation to a healing rod.

A power rod is usually held as you would grip any other type of tool. You can visualize and form the energy sphere beforehand. Visualization of the beam of energy projecting from the point of the crystal is also advisable. A visualization of a white-light energy, aura-type shield or field of energy can also be used to protect the operator from any kind of negative feedback reaction if the operator feels it is necessary. The shield visualization might be advisable if the operator is sending energy to a toxic chemical or radioactive area, for instance. It should be remembered that the thoughts for direction of the beam of energy and the emotions for amplification of the energy beam are necessary for successful operation of a crystal power rod.

Intense desire and thought pictures with unconditional love as a motivating factor can prove to be a very powerful force for accomplishing the desired effect. A clear visualization of the goal by the rod operator is extremely helpful, although a general energy balancing and healing can also be projected. In many cases where the subject is an area of Mother Earth, the energy can be projected in an unqualified manner. This leaves the decision to use a particular effect of the healing energy up to the Earth Mother herself.

The energy beam can be visualized as reaching out thousands of miles across the Earth, or it can be seen as traveling at about a six-foot altitude through the geomagnetic field that surrounds the planet. The beam of the power rod can also be seen as arcing from one point on the Earth to another point, like a rainbow across the sky. In fact, remembering that the white-light beam includes all the healing colors of the rainbow is a good practice for understanding the beneficial effects of the energy. The crystal energy beam can also be seen as traveling straight through the Earth, since the energy on a subatomic level moves through all forms of matter as easily as it moves through air or water.

It's good to remember that the power rod's beam of energy is more than just a visualization of energy that follows thought. This practice is a form of perception that human beings are beginning to redevelop or reawaken again, and it allows us to see ourselves as the energy beings that we really are. It's usually not long after projecting a beam of energy from a crystal rod that the operator begins to see the white-light beam coming out of a white-light sphere or oval.

This egg-shaped aura is not just an aura of the person; it is a reflection of the spirit and true nature of humans as energy beings who are within manifested physical bodies. Seeing this leads to a much wider understanding of the fluid nature of the wide variety of energy fields that are interdependent within the energy field of the planet. This is the energy field of the Universe itself.

Through the use of crystals and energy rods, the doors of self and the Universe continue to open or unfold between the interpenetrating energy fields or dimensions.

MINIATURE MAGNETIC POWER HEALING ROD

This rod combines the magnetic and crystal forces, and it is a very popular model, since it can be used as either a healing rod or a power rod. It uses ½-inch copper pipe with a copper cap on one end and a ¾- to

Miniature Magnetic Power/ Healing Rod

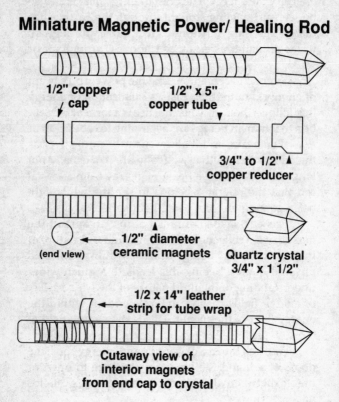

1/2" copper cap

1/2" x 5" copper tube

3/4" to 1/2" copper reducer

1/2" diameter ceramic magnets

(end view)

Quartz crystal 3/4" x 1 1/2"

1/2 x 14" leather strip for tube wrap

Cutaway view of interior magnets from end cap to crystal

½-inch reducer for a crystal mount on the other end. The magnetic force is provided by loading ½-inch diameter magnets from the end cap to the crystal. It uses a larger size quartz crystal fitted in the large end of the reducer with leather or copper mesh shims and glue for attachment. The leather wrap is done in the new style with the cap and reducer left exposed. It is still small enough to be carried in a pocket or a purse.

Operation is the same as the other rods, using mental visualization amplified by an emotional feeling of love. Refer to the drawing for the specifications of parts.

DOUBLE T-LODESTONE
POWER HEALING ROD
(Pocket Size)

This is another dual-purpose rod, with an added energy boost of natural magnetic lodestone combined with a double termination quartz crystal. The crystal is mounted in the new style with a ½-inch copper coupler. The end cap and the coupler are left uncovered when the leather wrap is glued on. This is another pocket or purse size that is handy to carry. Many people prefer the natural lodestone magnetic energy over the manmade ceramic magnets.

The operating procedure is the same as the other rods, with the major emphasis on healing uses. The color of the leather wrap is usually chosen with the personal healing color in mind. Purple or green seem to be the most popular colors for this one. It is also advisable to obtain the clearest double termination quartz crystal with very few chips or flaws. None are really flawless, but quite a few in the ½-inch diameter by 1¼-inch length size are excellent specimens. These are quite suitable for this type of rod. The

Double Terminated, Lodestone Power/ Healing Rod

POCKET SIZE

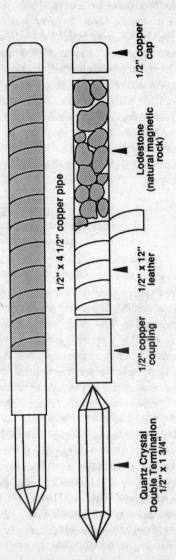

1/2" x 4 1/2" copper pipe

1/2" copper cap

Lodestone (natural magnetic rock)

1/2" x 12" leather

1/2" copper coupling

Quartz Crystal Double Termination 1/2" x 1 3/4"

overall length is about 5¾ inches.

QUARTZ CRYSTAL FILLED POWER ROD

This is called a power rod, and indeed it is. It is good to remember that only the most powerful people can afford to be gentle. Any power rod is, by its very nature, also a healing rod. This one is filled with quartz crystals and crystal chips. If you've done many crystal projects, you will usually have many tiny crystals and assorted chips left over. If you load these into the copper pipe of a rod and pack them tightly, you will have a crystal rod, literally. This one is medium size, between pocket and standard size, approximately eight inches in length. The energy field or beam from this many quartz crystals is rather intense. The crystals enjoy being next to each other instead of being discarded. We would feel the same way.

It is constructed in the new style with the crystal mounted in a copper coupler. The coupler and the end cap are left uncovered, while the center section of the rod is leather wrapped as usual. (Refer to the drawing for specifications.)

IRON OXIDE AND QUARTZ-FILLED HEALING POWER ROD

This rod is similar to the quartz-filled rod, except that it is filled with a natural mix of small quartz crystals and iron oxide as it is found in crystal mines. I use a mix from the Arkansas mines. This is easier to acquire because many rock shops in the United States have it left over as residue from cleaning their larger crystal specimens. The other difference in this rod is that it is almost the standard length, about 11 to 12 inches, but is a smaller diameter, using ½-inch diameter copper pipe. (Refer to the drawing for specifications.)

Quartz Crystal Filled Power Rod

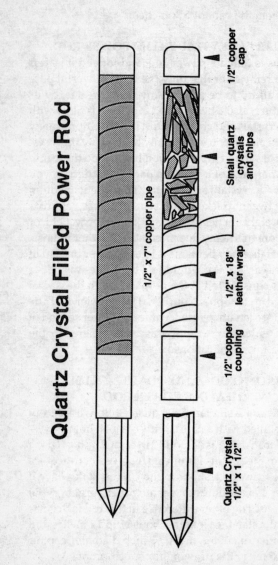

1/2" x 7" copper pipe

1/2" copper cap

Small quartz crystals and chips

1/2" x 18" leather wrap

1/2" copper coupling

Quartz Crystal 1/2" x 1 1/2"

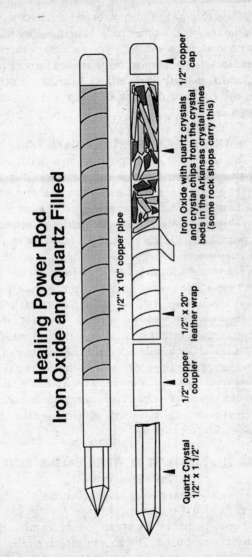

Healing Power Rod
Iron Oxide and Quartz Filled

1/2" x 10" copper pipe

1/2" copper cap

Iron Oxide with quartz crystals and crystal chips from the crystal beds in the Arkansas crystal mines (some rock shops carry this)

1/2" x 20" leather wrap

1/2" copper coupler

Quartz Crystal 1/2" x 1 1/2"

Again, this is a healing power rod, and it is used in the same way as the other rods. Like the other filled rods, no matter how carefully you pack them, there is a slight loose rattle in most cases. It has a heavier feel to it, which many people enjoy. As with the other rods, the color of the leather wrap is a personal preference.

SHORT LARGE CRYSTAL POWER ROD

This is one of the most popular models. It is standard size diameter (¾-inch copper pipe). It is cut down to pocket size with the quartz crystal mounted in the new style. The quartz crystal, as clear and with as few chips as possible, is mounted in the ¾-inch copper coupler using leather or copper mesh for shims, which are attached securely with instant bonding glue. The center section is a 4½-inch length of ¾-inch copper pipe. The overall length is approximately six inches, depending on the length of the crystal used. A ¾-inch copper end cap is used. The leather is wrapped on the center section, only the cap and the coupler are left exposed. A popular color of leather to use is black, since the contrast with the copper is so well defined, but any color may be used. This is a heavy-duty, star warrior type energy force rod. It operates the same as the others, with focused thought and amplified emotions.

LARGE AMETHYST POWER HEALING ROD
(Traditional Style)

This rod is constructed full length using a 12-inch piece of ¾-inch diameter copper pipe. Overall length can be up to 14 inches. depending on the length of the amethyst crystal used. The copper pipe is slotted in order to fit the crystal, with leather pieces and glue

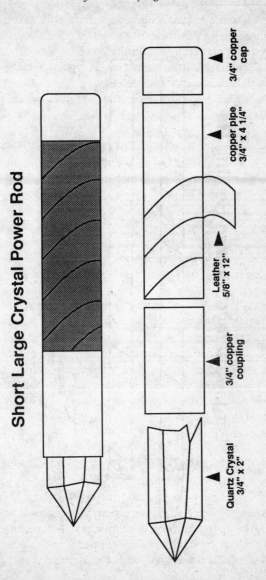

Short Large Crystal Power Rod

3/4" copper cap

copper pipe
3/4" x 4 1/4"

Leather
5/8" x 12"

3/4" copper
coupling

Quartz Crystal
3/4" x 2"

Large Amethyst Power/ Healing Rod
TRADITIONAL STYLE

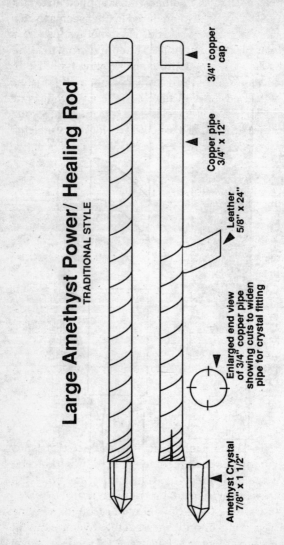

3/4" copper cap

Copper pipe
3/4" x 12"

Leather
5/8" x 24"

Enlarged end view
of 3/4" copper pipe
showing cuts to widen
pipe for crystal fitting

Amethyst Crystal
7/8" x 1 1/2"

used to attach it. The leather wrap is applied up to and around the crystal. Green or red leather seems to be a favorite for this type of rod. The amethyst can be a deep purple to a light violet. The energy from this one is of a calm, peaceful, protective healing type with a good balance. These can easily be built in the smaller size if desired. As with all rods, if there is a change or modification that you feel is right for you, follow your feeling and construct it exactly the way you want it for your personal use.

THE CRYSTAL LIGHT BEACON

This is a construction that can be used for psionic experiments or as a decoration. It is an excellent way to utilize crystals that you feel may not be suitable for many of the other experiments but are still of too high a quality to dismiss. (Refer to diagram for construction.)

Materials

- A. Double or single termination quartz crystal— clear, cloudy or smoky, 2" x 4"
- B. Leather wrap or copper strip, 2" wide
- C. Brass shell case or copper cylinder, 12" x 2"
- D. Brass or copper base, 3" diameter
- E. Copper wire wrap, if leather is used

The Crystal Light Beacon is a device that lends itself to various uses: meditating, sending and receiving white-light energy, or transmitting and receiving Universal Energy from the Universe itself.

It can be used as an energy beacon for sending and receiving energy messages between sentient beings throughout the Universe or for sending mental

Crystal Light Beacon

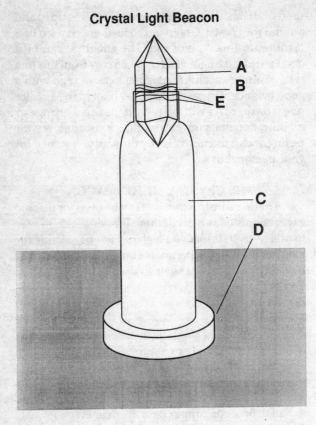

and emotional messages to people on our planet. It also is effective for sending healing energy to the Earth Mother. One of its most positive uses is to send a blessing to the spirit, mineral, plant, winged and water people, including our four-legged and two-legged brothers and sisters.

We can all benefit from this sending of good energy, whether we are the senders or receivers.

4   The Pyramid and the Crystal

"There is no substitute for self-inspiration."

CRYSTAL ENERGY DOORS

The brown-skinned man moved silently through the South American jungle. The Sun's rays through the treetops reflected off the blue-feathered headdress he wore. The feathers were not really blue but refracted light from the sky and so appeared that color. The headdress had been passed down through the generations, coming from his great-great grandfather who, it was said, came here from the land across the big water to the east where the Sun rose. He carried something else that had been passed through the generations as well. In the fur bag slung over his shoulder was a shiny copper pyramid with a clear crystal pointing out from the top. He could not understand why the copper was considered so much more valuable than the gold and silver that adorned the stonework of the ancient jungle cities, yet he treasured this sacred object as his father had before him. He did understand that when he reached the rare, pointed gray stone pyramid at the magic spot in the jungle and put the copper cap on it, mysterious things happened.

During the day this priest-healer with the blue-feathered headdress sat by the pyramid and played a carved wooden flute. The early evening would reverberate with his drumbeats like the heartbeats of the Universal Creator. As night darkened the jungle around the pyramid, the crystal on the copper cap began to glow with a blue-white light. The pyramid itself shimmered with an aura outlined with a white light that sometimes reflected the colors of the rainbow. A bright star appeared in the dark sky above the pyramid. As it came lower, a circle of light brighter than the Sun, it lit up the jungle around the ancient stonework. Later when the rays of the morning Sun pierced the thick foliage, the gray stone structure sat silent, darkened and abandoned. There were no signs of a man with blue feathers, a flute, a drum or a copper crystal cap. It was as if they had never been there. Yet after over 5,000 years, the man of the blue feathers would return to awaken the sacred spot's energy with his drumbeat shaking the jungle.

Meanwhile, in another world . . . .

A young lady in a white lab coat stood gazing at the square of copper with the crystals on the corners angled inward and upward. She thought she saw a fine line of bluish light being emitted from each crystal, but she wasn't sure. Her gaze followed the lines of light to where they intersected at the point of the crystal on the end of the center copper column. The shape of the light lines formed a perfect energy light pyramid, invisible and not invisible at the same time. It couldn't really exist, yet the plants sitting within the invisible line of the pyramid were growing just fine. A week before, she had taken out the previous test plants, and they had dried out. The two opposite reactions to the same test were puzzling. There was more going on here than first suspected, and she was going to continue exploring this energy phenomenon until she found out what was going on.

DOUBLE PYRAMID CRYSTAL
ENERGY POWERHOUSE

The exact use of this double pyramid type device has not been determined yet. It is a very powerful generator of energy. Please use common sense in experiments with this.

Parts

A. 5/8" x 10½" wood circle for the base

B. Two ½" copper caps, bolted inside top and bottom of pyramid

C. Two ½" reducers and two 1" lengths of ½" copper tube for the top and bottom crystal mounts

D. Six 3/8" x 1" natural quartz crystals for the top, bottom and four corners of the two pyramids

E. Eight ½" x 8" copper or brass straps

F. One 5½" x 5½" x ¼" wood square over one 5½" x 5½" copper square

G. One 1" diameter or larger natural quartz crystal sphere

H. One ½" copper cap on hanger

I. Two 2" bolts and nuts for attaching top and bottom caps to strap and hanger

J. One 4" x ½" copper pipe for hanger

K. One ½" copper coupling

L. One ½" copper elbow

M. One 10" x ½" copper pipe for hanger upright

N. One ½" copper coupling for base mount

Construction: Double Pyramid Form

1. Cut a 5½" square of copper.
2. Cut a 5½" square of wood.

Double Pyramid Crystal Energy Powerhouse

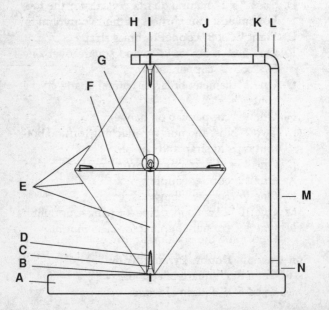

3. Cut eight ½" x 8" copper or brass straps.

4. Bend straps to shape a pyramid with a 6" base and 5⅞" sides.

5. Drill five holes—one bolt-sized hole in each corner of the copper and wood squares ½" inside each corner, and one ½" hole in the center of the squares.

6. Round the corners of the squares.

7. Fit straps of pyramid shape to the squares, bending the straps in across the bolt holes in the corners. Cut off the excess strap and drill the holes for bolts.

8. Drill holes for the bolts in the center of the two copper caps and bolt the caps to the apex, then reform the pyramid shape.

9. Attach quartz crystals and reducers to the top and bottom caps.

10. Bolt strap sides to the wood and copper squares.

Construction: Base and Hanger

1. Cut a 10½" circle of wood, ⅝" thick.

2. An optional ⅝" copper or brass strap can be attached to the edge of the circle base for decoration.

3. Drill the center ¼" hole in the circle for the bottom apex bolt to fit in.

4. Drill a ½" hole, one inch from the edge of the circle for the copper coupling and the 10" upright to fit in, and set it upright.

5. Place the elbow and the 4" x ½" copper pipe on the 10" upright.

6. Determine the position for the bolt hole in the 4" pipe to hold the structure straight up. Then drill the hole for the top bolt and attach the pipe.

7. Place the ½" copper cap on the end of the pipe.
8. Recheck and adjust so that the double pyramid is straight and level.
9. Place the other four quartz crystals at the corners of the wood and copper square with the points facing inward towards the center hole.
10. Set the crystal sphere in the center hole.

The device is now complete.

This shape forms two pyramids from tip to tip, so it does not have an outlet for energy. This means that the crystal sphere in the center is constantly building up a charge of energy. It is suggested that the crystal sphere (or the other crystals) be removed when it is not in use to avoid a buildup of too much energy with no outlet. Your personal judgment should be used in this matter. This unit is far more powerful than it appears.

INVISIBLE PYRAMID ENERGY QUARTZ CRYSTAL GENERATOR

This device derives the shape of a pyramid from the points of the crystals. This is usually visualized by the operator and formed of invisible energy, although some people who are sensitive to energies can see the pyramid form outlined in blue-white or other colors.

Parts

    A. One 18" x 18" square copper sheet
    B. One ½" copper cap and mounting bolt
    C. One 15 ¼" x ½" copper pipe upright
    D. One copper reducer, ¾" to ½"
    E. One quartz crystal, ½" x 1"
    F. Four quartz crystals, ½" x 2"

Invisible Pyramid Energy Generator

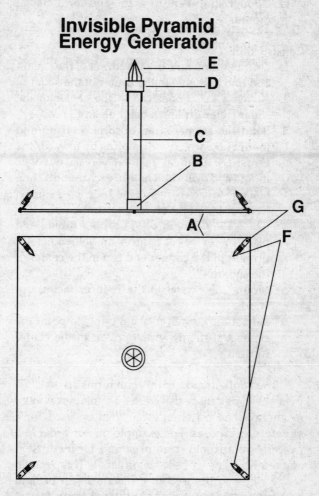

G. Copper strap bent to shape and form crystal mounts.

Construction

1. Drill a ¼" bolt hole in each corner of the square and one bolt hole in the center of the square.
2. Attach a ½" copper cap to the center of the square after drilling a bolt hole in the cap.
3. Bend the copper strap to form a clamp and mount for each crystal pointing up towards the center at a diagonal. Take each crystal out of its mount and drill a bolt hole in each mount. Then bolt one to each corner of the 18" copper square. Remount the four crystals securely.
4. Cut a 15½" length of ½" copper tubing and place the ½" x ¾" reducer on one end; set it upright in the copper end cap in the center of the square.
5. Mount the crystal in the reducer facing upwards.
6. Adjust the corner crystal mounts to point the crystals at the tip of the crystal in the center upright.

The configuration of this unit forms an invisible pyramid energy shape that creates a significant amount of energy. The psi energy can then be used for a variety of purposes. For example, it can provide a peaceful aura (room-sized or larger) for meditation and receiving energy-based information. This pyramid shape can also be used to project a beam of light energy from the top crystal point for sending information or healing energy.

INVISIBLE PYRAMID ENERGY
CRYSTAL SPHERE DEVICE

Like the model with the crystal point, this device with the crystal ball can be used to send or receive energy. It can also be used to create an energy aura of a peaceful sanctuary over a large area such as a house.

Two separate pyramid devices can be built, or one base unit like the one on p. 67 can be adapted for use by replacing the copper reducer on top of the upright with a ½" copper coupling and setting the 1" diameter crystal sphere on top of the coupling.

Do not attach either the coupling or the reducer permanently, so that the base unit can be used for either device economically without building two separate units.

The purpose of these units is variable, depending on the operator. The type of energy produced is also a subject of heated debate. Many people have expressed the view that a crystal point projects a beam and a crystal ball radiates a field or aura of energy. Others take the opposite viewpoint. They use the crystal ball for projecting a beam and the crystal point for radiating an aura or field. My experience is that either a crystal ball or a point can produce either a beam or a field of energy depending on the person using the crystal or crystal device.

Both devices are capable of generating a lot of energy and should be treated with adequate respect.

PYRAMID ENERGY AMPLIFIER

There are some larger pyramid frames on the market in three-, five- and six-foot sizes. Since these prefabricated pyramids are available, it makes it easy to adapt crystals to them (including the pyramid cap mentioned later on.). The other advantage of the larger sizes is that you can sit inside them or hang them from the ceiling so that your head will be in the pyramid while you sit in a chair. The following device requires a prefabricated pyramid in the six-foot size mentioned above, and it uses a crystal attached to the apex to intensify the energy of the pyramid.

PYRAMID WITH BASE AND FIXED DOUBLE TERMINATION CRYSTAL

Materials

A. A prefabricated pyramid with six-foot base (or a home-built model). The prefabricated models are manufactured with and without a clear plastic covering. Either variety will do. These come without the base frame section shown in the diagram.

B. Copper wire in spiral wrap (insulated or bare wire)

C. Quartz crystal, double termination with copper wire wrapped around it to connect it to the pyramid apex

D. Base frame section—four to five ½" pieces of wood to connect corners of pyramid

PYRAMID WITHOUT BASE WITH HANGING SINGLE TERMINATION CRYSTAL

E. Open frame prefabricated pyramid without base frame

F. Copper wire lead and hanger to crystal for king's chamber position connected to frame spirals at apex

G. Quartz crystal, single termination (one pointed, optional)

Pyramid Energy Amplifier

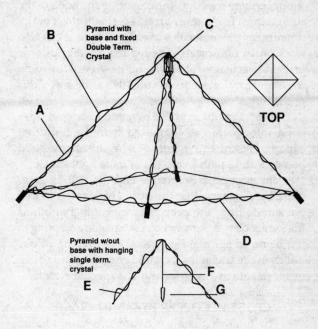

Pyramid with base and fixed Double Term. Crystal

B

C

A

D

TOP

Pyramid w/out base with hanging single term. crystal

E

F

G

The open frame version of the pyramid with no base frame sides has been used in recent experiments with a hanging single termination crystal for auto energizing. The apex of the pyramid and crystal should be centered over the engine on the hood of the automobile. The reason for this is that if this energy can rebuild the molecules of a razor blade, it can also work on larger objects. The reports of other psionic machines actually materializing new parts in some large electrical systems also tends to reinforce this procedure.

Some general study of pyramid energy and related information is suggested before attempting experiments of this nature. There are many good books dealing with pyramids in most bookstores.

The process is so simple and the materials required are so basic that the main challenge is to free our minds from the preconceived complex notions that our society has grown accustomed to accepting in the name of so-called progress. The freeing of our minds in the use of the pyramid energy amplifier can produce some wonderful and unexpected results.

CRYSTAL COPPER PYRAMID FRAME

The following is a basic copper pyramid frame with a stand and legs. The rod extension on the top can be lengthened or shortened to meet your needs and perception. This frame can be used for meditation, pyramid, crystal and psi experiments. Let your intuition and imagination be your guide.

Materials
   A. Quartz crystal, ¾" x 1½"
   B. Copper reducer, ¾" x 1"
   C. Copper pipe, ¾" x 2"

Crystal Copper
Pyramid Frame

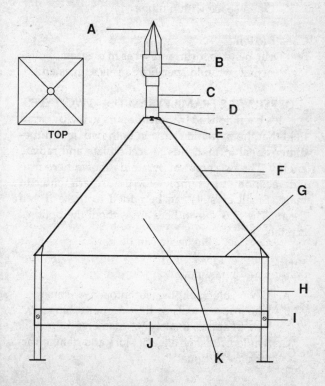

D. Copper cap, ¾"
E. Bolt to attach cap to apex
F. Four copper straps for pyramid frame, 8¾" length by ½" width of at least ³⁄₃₂" thickness
G. Pyramid base, copper sheet, 10" x 10" square
H. Four stand-frame legs, copper straps 5½" length by ½" width of at least ³⁄₃₂" thickness (can be one piece extended from pyramid frame)
I. Four bolts to attach leg frame support
J. Four leg frame supports, ½" wide copper strap by 10" lengths
K. Open space within frame

Construction

Drill, bend to form, and set as in diagram; building to actual pyramid specifications is suggested.

COPPER WIRE FRAME PYRAMIDS—TWO TYPES

It's been noticed by practitioners in the pyramid field that the pyramid shape in both two- and three-dimensional forms tends to accumulate and radiate energy. The two types of pyramids shown here provide economical examples for the experimenter to build. Small crystals can be added to these if you desire. The two shown here are without the optional crystals.

Parts

(Type 1—top view)
A. 2" x 6" block of pine, cut into a 5½" square
B. Four copper nails or thin copper tubing, 3½" long of approximately ¼" diameter
C. Sanded, finished edge of block and stain or varnish are optional

Copper Wire Frame Pyramids

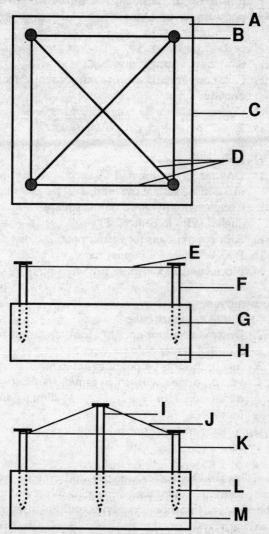

D. Small gauge bare copper wire strung to nails to form a two-dimensional pyramid between copper uprights on frame

(Type 1—side view)
E. Side view, copper wire
F. Four copper nails, one in each corner ½" from outside
G. Copper nails in ¾" hole drilled in block
H. 2" x 6" pine block cut to 5½" square

(Type 2—side view)
I. One larger center nail in second model for three-dimensional pyramid, 4½" height
J. Copper wire pyramid frame, square base and angled sides to center nail
K. Four copper nails for corner post, 2¼" height
L. Five ¾" holes for copper nails
M. Block base, 2" x 6" pine cut 5½" square

Construction
1. Cut 5½" square base.
2. Drill ¾" holes for uprights, four in corners for type 1, a center hole for type 2.
3. Insert uprights by pounding in gently.
4. Wind copper wire to pyramid shape, two-dimensional for type 1 and three-dimensional for type 2.

Optional: Sand and finish base to personal preference.

This is a very basic shape pyramid exercise with limited but entertaining uses, depending on the builder-operator. For instance, this device could be used for charging a crystal or other small objects set in the base.

Your imagination and intuition will lead you to other uses for this device.

COPPER CRYSTAL PYRAMID CAP

This was one of the most important secrets of the ancient priesthood, used to complete and operate the giant stone pyramids around the Earth.

This works as a unit by itself or acts as a super energy accumulator or amplifier when placed on a larger pyramid shape.

Materials

A. Quartz crystal, clear, unchipped facets
B. Copper cap, ½" diameter
C. Copper sheet cut to pyramid specifications—6" base, 5⅞" sides and 5" height
D. Four copper strap braces, drilled and attached with eight metal screws
E. One ¾" center cap, drilled and bolted, then soldered inside copper cap
F. Center cap screw, soldered in apex of pyramid for stability
G. Copper inverted cone for crystal and apex cover, optional (a brass or copper candle holder top may be used)

Construction

As described above, but modifications can be made, if desired, with material substitutions.

Pyramid Specifications:
  Base line: 6" per side
  Side angles: 5⅞"
  Height of trangle: approximately 5"

Copper Crystal Pyramid Cap

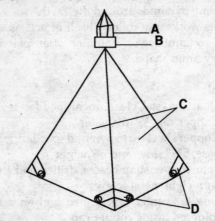

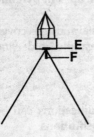

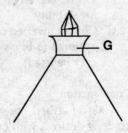

5 Car Crystals for Guidance and Balance

"Any rock or mineral can be used for any purpose you can visualize or think of."

The car crystal is important because we spend a considerable amount of time in our cars. We need the balance of energy we can achieve with a quartz crystal or cluster in an automobile, because our minds are usually concentrated on where we are going and when we need to be there.

A car crystal may be just one crystal, but like crystals anywhere else, it usually won't stay alone for very long. One crystal sitting in the console of an automobile will soon be surrounded by other crystals and assorted rocks or minerals of various types, colors and materials. This circle of crystal and mineral friends seems to come together miraculously from rock shops, river beds, roads, mountains or other places during the course of travel. The basic requirement for this arrangement, like all others, is that it feels good.

The reported uses of car crystals is constantly growing. Some of these are:

1. Programming the quartz to radiate an energy shield or field to protect the car and occupants from harm.
2. Healing and balancing the automobile in the energy and subatomic particle spectrum and

creating more reliable operation with better gas mileage.

3. Programming a crystal for guidance so that you will be where you are supposed to be at the right time. This is a good system to use when you're looking for rocks or minerals. Just pick up a seed rock from the area you're looking in, place it with your car crystals and hold one of them, usually a quartz or amethyst crystal, while asking it to guide you to the kind of rocks or minerals you are seeking. It's a good practice to keep an open mind after asking for guidance. This can lead to a mountain road a few miles off the main highway, a riverbed right beside where you're already parked, or even a rock and mineral shop in the next town 20 miles down the road. Anything is possible or probable with a locked-on car crystal guidance system. Awareness by the operator is a key factor for tuning in to being in the right place at the right time to find what you are seeking. This method can also be applied when seeking ideas, information, people or growth experiences.

4. A car crystal with its group of friendly crystals and rocks provides a constant connection or ground to the Earth Mother's source of nurturing. This in itself creates an automobile environment of healthy energy balancing, even if no specific programming for a purpose is involved.

5. Another important benefit of the car crystal circle is that they are pretty to look at and fun to play with while traveling.

6 The Crystal Experimenter

"Most other beings, like crystals, do not speak our human languages."

In crystal experiments various questions, ideas, modifications and other apparently unrelated data arise. I say apparently unrelated because it looks that way at first. Later on it usually fits into something that turns out to be useful. In this chapter I have included this type of information.

CUT, FACETED OR POLISHED QUARTZ CRYSTAL EXPERIMENT

This experiment came about because of a difference in opinion as to whether cut, faceted or polished quartz crystals still retained the energy characteristics of natural, uncut crystals. There is still a difference of opinion on this, although an uncut crystal does act as an energy charger for the cut or polished crystal.

As in all the experiments, only natural quartz crystals are used—no synthetic or leaded ones.

Materials

    A. 4" x 12" x ½" wood base with rounded corners

    B. Copper or brass clamp mount for disc

    C. Natural quartz crystal, uncut

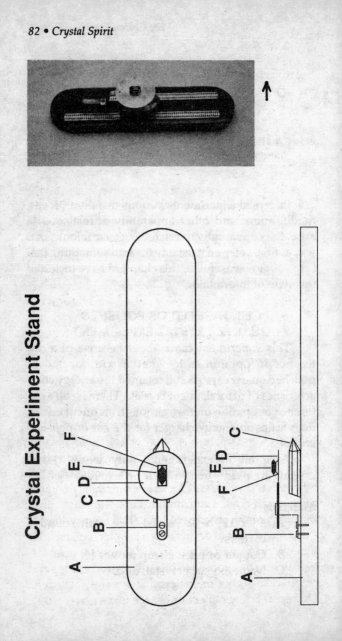

Crystal Experiment Stand

D. Copper or brass disc, 2½" in diameter
E. ½" x ⅜" cut, faceted, or polished natural quartz crystal
F. Silver stand for cut crystal, ¼" x ¼" x ½", bent to hold crystal

Construction

1. Cut wood base with rounded corners, 4" x ½" x 12".
2. Drill and mount copper or brass strap mount to wood base at 1½" height, about 4" in and centered on base. (Disc should be centered six inches in from end of wood base.)
3. Place uncut quartz crystal under disc, centered.
4. Bend ½" strip of silver in an oval shape to act as a stand for the cut crystal, and set it in the center of the disc.

Optional: One-half inch brass or copper strips can be attached to the edge of the base or attached to the top for decoration.

Any type of jewelry or stone can be charged or cleared by placing it with a quartz crystal. This can be done with or without a stand to charge them on. A charging stand can also be much simpler than the one used in this experiment: another rock, a board, a piece of cloth, the ground or a table top can all be used. Anywhere that crystals and rocks are together, they will renew each other and communicate with each other through the interchange of Universal Energy. This is the same thing that occurs when jewelry, crystals and other personal items are placed in the center of a healing circle to be exposed to blessings, good energy and positive thoughts or feelings. The same beneficial Universal Energy effect or charge takes place.

SHRINK-TUBE TYPE CRYSTAL
MOUNTING OR COVERING

Shrink tubing was originally intended for covering computer cables and wires. It shrinks to fit when heat is applied. An industrial heat gun is not necessary for heating shrink tubing. A butane lighter works well for short pieces, and the burner or heating element on a stove works for longer pieces.

Materials and Construction

A. Quartz crystal, clear tip with unchipped facets. Use shrink tube slightly larger than crystal. Heat to fit, cut away lower center part at crystal base.
B. Another covering a larger section of crystal higher up. Cut away center base section.
C. Another covering just a minimum of the crystal base with center cut away. (A variety of colors—red, blue, yellow—can be used other than the standard black shrink tube.)

This covering can be used to conceal any flaws in the lower section of the crystal. The other main use is to provide a protective cover as a shim for fitting the crystal into a copper tube or base for many of the experiments involved with quartz crystal.

This has been found to be just as effective as the original leather covering and shims, while being much easier to use. Plastic electrical tape has also been found to be useful but certainly does not look as good for exterior use.

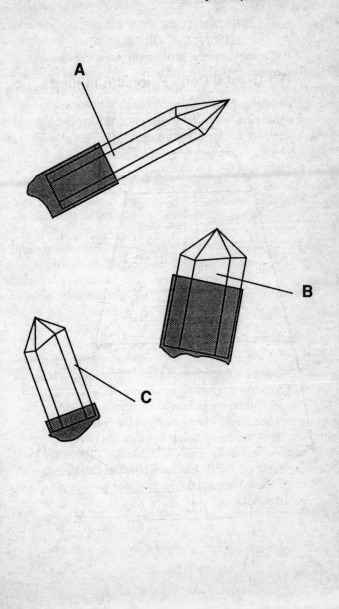

Tri-Crystal Cone Psionic Amplifier

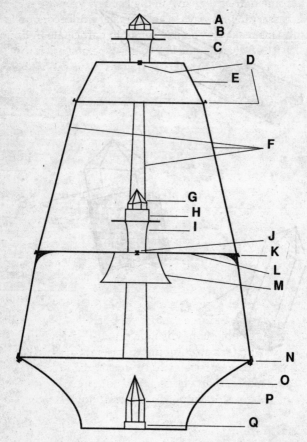

TRI-CRYSTAL CONE PSIONIC AMPLIFIER

This crystal device provides a way to use three smaller crystals for the same purpose as the large crystal communicator. The larger quartz crystals have become more expensive in the last few years, so it is necessary to find ways to keep crystal work economical. This makes it possible for all to participate in it.

The fact is that the key to this type of work is the consciousness of the person doing it. This cannot be emphasized too much.

Materials

A. Quartz crystal, ¾" x 1½"
B. Brass or copper ring crystal holder
C. Copper flange-cone, 1½" x 1"
D. Bolts for frame
E. Copper dish, inverted, 5½" diameter
F. Copper support frame—three struts, ½" wide strap, 12" long and at least ³⁄₃₂" thick
G. Middle quartz crystal, 1" x 2"
H. Brass or copper ring crystal holder
I. Copper flange-cone
J. Flange-dish-cone bolt mount
K. Strut-support strap, copper/with bolt
L. One of three middle supports
M. Copper cone-dish, inverted, 4" diameter
N. Bolt for strut mount to base of copper dish
O. Copper base dish, 10" to 12" diameter
P. Base quartz crystal, 1¼" x 2"
Q. Brass or copper base crystal holder/ring

Construction

As shown in diagram, but many variations can be used and the device will still be quite workable.

Model Shown:

11½" diameter base dish with a total height of 17".

The uses for this device are many and varied depending on the research and operator. This is an especially high-powered supermind amplifier. It is similar to the Beacon but is very useful with an operation of two, four, or six people acting as a circle in unison for a very powerful sending or receiving.

7 The Computer, the Crystal and the Black Box

"Miracles need to be made more practical and brought back down to earth."

This chapter is for those of you who have a basic working knowledge of black boxes or psionic generators. For those who don't know, a black box is a machine with electronic parts for amplifying the thoughts and emotions of the operator. The experiment below involves the use of a black box in conjunction with a computer and a crystal.

Since you're reading this, you probably have had some experience with quartz crystals. More than likely you've had some experience with computers in a business or at home. It's easy to combine these areas with psionic generators (black boxes) if this combination interests you. In order to understand this chapter, all that you need is a basic knowledge of simple psionic machines. For a good introduction to psionics you might try *Psychic Power* by Charles W. Cosimano (Llewellyn Publications, 1987). Another good handbook is *The Black Box and Other Psionic Generators* by W. E. Davis. (This is available from Lor'd Industries Ltd., Box 156, Hancock, WI 54943.)

The working knowledge necessary in this area is easy to obtain in a short period of time. It can also be quite fun and exciting.

PSICOM (P) OPERATION

The computer interface does not change the operating procedure for the psionic generator/radionic black box in any way. It does augment and amplify the regular operating procedure and the operator's thoughts and emotions, adding a program of more exacting accuracy for enhancing the normal operation.

Two methods have been utilized for the interface use:

(1) Program the computer before tuning the psionic generator, and
(2) Program the computer after tuning the psionic generator.

Either procedure will work, depending on the operator's preference.

Programming the computer to augment the psionic operator's thoughts and emotions: Use one screen of characters only. Do not put these instructions into a stored memory, or if you do, erase it immediately after the use of the psionic machine, whether the use takes hours, days or weeks.

The typed-in instructions on the screen should match the operator's thoughts as closely as possible. If necessary, use abbreviations to get the psionic imprint/instructions on just one screen of characters (visible on the computer screen at all times during the operation of the psionic generator). This holds the operator's thought instructions for the desired effect in a more stable, usable and accurate form for extended periods of time. This will enhance the effective operation of any type or model of psionic or radionic machine.

The key factors for successful operation are still dependent on the operator's concentration and visualization, combined with sensitivity, ability, practice

and experience.

These machines enhance and augment these factors to an incredible degree with the most advanced synthesis of ancient and modern techniques.

QUARTZ CRYSTAL AMPLIFIED
COPPER TRANSFER SCREEN
FOR HOME COMPUTER INTERFACE
WITH PSIONIC GENERATOR

Materials

    A. 1″ x 12″ x 12″ wood frame to fit in front of a small screen TV or video display terminal

    B. Copper wire screen grid, ¼″ square

    C. Copper lead wires (insulated)

    D. Copper lead wires (insulated)

E. Plastic or glass dome, 3" diameter x 4" or 5" height
F. Copper wire lead contact for crystal tip
G. Quartz crystal, 3" x 1" or larger diameter, clear, unchipped facets
H. Wood or plastic control box (size variable)
I. ¾" x 5" x 5" wood frame to fit over the psionic generator sample plate
J. Copper lead wires, insulated
K. Copper screen wire grid for the psionic generator
L. Cord and plug for 110v warning light (the only direct electrical source) for regular wall outlet (optional)
M. Switch for warning light (optional)
N. Red warning light (optional)
O. Control knobs and four to six rheostats, variable capacitors or a combination of both types
P. Switches between O. above
Q. Capacitors, any size, between O. above

Construction

As described above, with personal variations on the basic pattern—i.e., copper wire grid can be modified or replaced with copper screen. The number and placement of rheostats and capacitors and variable capacitors can be adjusted according to personal preference of design.

The main wiring diagram is separate from the 110v power source for the warning light and not connected at all.

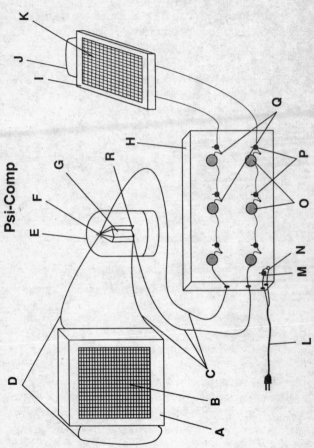

Psi-Comp

8 Crystal Power *Questions and Answers*

"A crystal cannot tell a human being anything he or she does not already know or have access to."

Since my prior book, *Crystal Power*, has become so popular, it has been impossible to answer all the questions in the overwhelming volume of letters I've received. The most adequate solution I've been able to provide is to read and record the many questions so that I can answer them in a special chapter of this book. This seems to be the best way to serve the needs of my brother and sister crystal people. It is with you in mind that this *Crystal Power* question section is written. I must add thanks to you all, since your input has helped me greatly.

1. *The use of glue with crystals.*

The use of glue in constructing quartz crystal devices does not seem to alter the energy characteristics of the crystals. The energy output and absorption appears to remain the same, probably since energy particles pass through most types of matter unhindered. Epoxy glues have been used with crystals and proved to be adequate. Silicon has also been used to mount crystals in rods, copper cups and quartzite rocks with satisfactory results and no harmful effects to the crystals or people.

The main effect to avoid with glue, water or salt water in relation to quartz crystals is rapid temperature changes that can cause cracking and breaking. Rapid temperature changes without water or glue on the surface can have the same effect.

In mounting, glue is usually only used on the lower part of the crystal, sides or base as a matter of aesthetics only.

2. *Different wraps for rods.*

The crystal rods were first wrapped with leather in the tradition of Native American crafts. It seemed that the leather acted as insulation, but this turned out not to be the case. Uncovered copper crystal rods function as well as those that are wrapped. Other wrappings have been used with success. PVC shrink tubing, plastic and rubber electrical tape, cloth and yarn, have all been substituted for the leather wrap with positive results.

Many variations in the way the crystal rods were wrapped have been used with success. Some rods have been built with the wrapping material covering one half of the copper tube at either end. Others have been wrapped with a handgrip in the middle of the rod, leaving both ends uncovered. All crystal rods with exposed copper still functioned properly.

The wrapping used on crystal energy rods is, most of all, a highly individual decision based on what the person building the rod feels good with. This usually starts with choosing a favorite color of wrap. If leather is used, the smooth side or the rougher suede-type side of the leather can be turned outward, depending on which side feels comfortable as well as what looks good to the person using the crystal rod.

3. *Decorations for the rods.*

The variety of crystal rods being made today, a decade and a half after their reinvention, is incredible to say the least. Some rods have been built and decorated Native American style with fur, feathers, and beadwork designs. Other rods have been built with bands of gold and silver added on as personal energy decorations. There are also rods that have been built of copper or silver and left unwrapped.

Various stones such as amethyst, rose quartz, turquoise, lapis, rubies and many others have been used to adorn the silver and copper rods. Some of these crystal rods now look like works of art, with the variation of stone patterns and elaborate designs abounding. Science, art and religion combine as one expression with the creation of crystal energy rods.

4. *Metals and other materials for crystal rods.*

Copper, silver or gold seems to work best for crystal rods, separately or in various combinations. Choices of metals are dependent on individual preference and, of course, individual economics. Copper is the most reasonably priced metal and has proven to be the most serviceable, as rods are exposed to regular daily use. Silver and gold work just as well, but no better than copper. Metal combinations, such as brass and bronze, have been used with equal success. Even platinum can be used if desired.

Most versions of the crystal energy rods are constructed using a hollow copper tube as an energy-particle chamber behind the crystal. It was soon discovered that the copper tube could be loaded with a wide variety of materials and still function as an amplification chamber.

Round magnets or small pieces of lodestone

placed in the copper tube add a complimentary energy field to the quartz crystal in the energy rod. This particular version is now one of the most popular models of the crystal rod in use today.

Rods also work well when loaded with smaller quartz crystals or crystal and quartz chips. Some have been filled with iron oxide and small crystals from the mine beds in Arkansas.

Many rods have been loaded with other quartz crystals using spacers to hold them in place, an inch apart, throughout the rod's entire length.

Other types of crystals and gemstones have also been used inside crystal energy rods with equal success. Such stones as rose quartz, jade, turquoise, aquamarine, malachite, citrine, amethyst, to name a few, have been used successfully with the crystal healing rods.

5. *Sizes of crystal rods and staffs.*

Practically every rod size imaginable has been built. Some have been as small as an inch in length by ⅛ inch in diameter with tiny quartz crystals. At the other end of the scale are staffs constructed of ¾-inch diameter copper over seven feet in length. Others have been built three feet long using two, four and six inch diameters with very large crystals (large for energy rods, that is). Everyone who builds crystal rods seems to find a size suitable for their individual use, a size they feel comfortable with.

Some crystal energy rods have been constructed using telescoping tubes so that their length can be adjusted for tuning the rod to the crystal or to the person operating the rods.

Many crystal experimenters have asked if a longer length, a larger diameter or a larger crystal produces more power or energy output. When speaking of the Universal Energy that comes through quartz crystals, the "bigger is better and more powerful" theory does not hold true. Even a tiny grain of quartz sand is part of the energy fields of the Universe.

The perception and conscious awareness of the operator is far more important than the size of the crystal or crystal energy rod. An aware, balanced person will produce a more powerful energy flow through a small crystal rod than a less aware person could produce from a giant energy staff. The person is the key. You and I are the deciding factor.

This is not to say that the same size crystal rod should be used by everyone or that there is one "right" size for all. Experimentation is necessary to determine the size rod that "feels" right for you personally. Individuals and crystals are all unique, with no two exactly the same.

It is sometimes true that an increase in the size of a rod or crystal can cause an increase in the power of energy output. It is also true that a decrease in the size of a rod or crystal can cause an increase in energy projection. This is a situation that is determined by balance and attunement of the crystal rod with its operator, which is an important consideration, perhaps the main factor involved.

When using more than one crystal in a rod, compatibility or balance between crystals by feel is definitely a condition to be aware of. Harmonious interaction of both energy fields and individual quartz crystals is as important as the interactions between individual people. In both cases energy fields of conscious beings are involved. This can be as complex or as simple as you want to make it. Keeping it simple is more fun.

This feeling of balanced energy interaction between crystals applies to rods that are loaded with several crystals inside as well as to the use of two or more rods together. It also applies to the use of crystals with other rocks, minerals and gemstones. Use your own judgment, as always.

6. *The crystals themselves.*

Choosing a quartz crystal for a crystal tool is a very personal, individual process for both the person and the crystal. Often a crystal chooses a person instead. More often, the person and the crystal "choose" each other, working together as they form a relationship of interacting energy fields. The coming together of a crystal and a person means more than just what feels good for the person, although feeling good energy is one part of the crystal relationship. The conscious beings involved in this interrelationship are the human being, the crystal being and the Earth herself. Good energy for one is good energy for all. Good energy relationships are what "being" is all about.

While we usually try to find quartz crystals for these crystal power tools that are symmetrical with clear, unchipped facets, this is not an absolute requirement. We would be in quite a sorry fix if the quartz crystals waited to choose human beings that looked perfect.

All crystals, regardless of what they look like, have the particular structure that is actively energy-connected to the rest of the Universe. Likewise, all people, regardless of their degree of awareness, are energy-connected to the Universe.

It should always be remembered that crystal beings respond to human beings exactly the way we think they do. Some people think a crystal point projects a beam of Universal Energy. It does. Others think a crystal point sends out a different field of energy. It does. Many people think a natural quartz crystal ball radiates a field of energy. It will.

Some people think a crystal ball sends out a beam of energy, and it will. There are people who think quartz crystal points and balls do nothing for them with energy at all. That is exactly what the crystals will do for them, nothing at all.

In the last 15 years we have learned that a lot of preconceptions we have had about crystals were actually misconceptions, coming from our own inflexible and narrow vision of awareness. As our awareness increased and widened, so did the characteristics of our crystal friends increase to the same degree.

We now see from experience that all crystals, minerals, rocks, gemstones and the Earth herself are working with us, not just for us. While we program and tune crystals, they are in turn tuning us to a larger Universal Energy frequency for the Earth Mother. Each member of the mineral kingdom of the Earth Mother is open and receptive to the emotion of love and the energy of thought.

Some people advise using crystals with various facets and shapes for specific uses. While this practice is good for many people, it does tend to make a simple activity into a complex one. Choosing crystals by what "feels right" is the easiest process, even if you pick up and hold crystals without looking at them or intellectually trying to decide which one is right for you or another.

Whether cloudy, milky, chipped, clear, cracked, double or single terminated, twinned, tripleted, clustered, angled, trenched, fused or included, the crystals themselves will tell you by a feeling if you're right for them or they're right for you. Quartz crystal beings will also tell you by feel if they want to be used in a copper and crystal tool, or if they want to be shaped into a ball, pyramid or egg, mounted in silver or gold jewelry. They'll even tell you if they wish to be cut or polished if you listen by feeling.

Our crystal friends also tell us when they want to be left as they are in their natural state. The elementals of the mineral kingdom are sometimes very forceful when telling us to leave them as they are. Some of the ways they tell us to leave them as they are can be dramatic if we're not listening closely. Disappearing or getting lost for periods of time or permanently is a forceful way of letting us know. Being very difficult to mount in jewelry or a crystal tool is another method they use if we don't catch on right away. Some crystals have been reported as frequently falling off necklaces and earrings as well as out of crystal rods until we finally get the message.

Likewise, the energy output depends on the operator's personal relationship to the crystal energy being. A weak or diffused energy projection reflects the crystal interrelationship of the individual, not a flaw in the crystal energy connection with universal forces.

It's often been asked if a power booster-amplifier can be built into a crystal energy rod. Coils of copper wire with capacitors and resistors and a switch with rheostats can be built into a rod, but this is like the autoelectromags in complexity. A simpler, more effective way to increase the force of a crystal rod's electromagnetic particle field or beam is by loading the rod with round ceramic magnets. For a more down-to-earth boost, insert lodestone or magnetite into a rod to balance the electromagnetic force with the crystal's energy field. Most crystals like this magnetic relationship, since it helps them grow and evolve or raise their own vibrations, consciousness and awareness. A series of single or double termination crystals also have an amplifying effect with or without magnetic materials.

7. *More about rods and staffs.*

The copper cap at one end of a crystal rod serves to define a particle or energy accumulation chamber as well as direct the flow of energy one way through a crystal and out the point. This is true whether the crystal is a single or a double termination.

On the other hand, mounting a crystal in each end of the copper tube forms an accumulation chamber for energy just as well. This was the form used for the original crystal healing rod of a decade and a half ago. Many healers still prefer this model today for the healing energy flow in both directions. This falls into the category of, "The healers balance in others what needs to be balanced in themselves," as well as, "teachers teaching others what they themselves need to learn."

As for two crystals—one in each end of the energy rod, single or double terminated or one of each type—all work equally well, depending on the "feel" of the person using the rod.

Crystal staffs are usually constructed with a crystal in only one end, since the natural inclination is to rest the other end on the ground. These can be built with a crystal in each end for use in martial arts methods of spiritual development in which neither end of the staff ever touches the floor or ground. The length of the staff—from the three-foot scepter to the four-, five-, six- and even seven-foot models—leaves a lot of room for personalization and decoration.

These additions to crystal staffs can be a simple

wrap of leather thongs and a sheepskin handgrip. Beadwork, feathers, gold, silver, copper rings and gemstones also have been set at various positions on the staff. This is determined by the staff builders themselves, with no limitations on imagination or experience. Many decorations, such as other crystals or stones, work energy in conjunction with the crystals mounted in the rods and staffs.

It has often been asked if variations in the designs of staffs can include wood as the main body of the power tool. Quite a number of innovative variations have been reported in the last decade. The mind of the builder-operator is the key component, since all types of tools work well.

Staffs have been made of wood with the crystal on one end and a copper cap at the other, with a copper wire spiral connecting the crystal and copper cap. These worked well, both with or without an insulating handgrip attached to the staff. Some have used copper or even carbon wire running through a hole in the center of the staff. Even wooden staffs with a crystal mounted on one end and no wire or copper cap have performed well with energy projections. The "feel" of the operator has proven to be the determining factor time and time again.

The original staff model of the early 1970s was just a longer version of the crystal power rod, using ¾-inch copper tubing, cap and the standard leather wrap. Like the rods, staffs can be loaded with other crystals, magnets and minerals. Other wrapping materials can also be used.

8. *Crystal power headbands and other communicators.*

Copper is normally used for crystal power tools because it conducts a smooth flow of energy. Gold, silver or even platinum will work as well but are much more expensive.

Many variations of the crystal power headband are now in use. Some people use the original design with the copper band going part way around the operator's head and the adjustable tie lace in back. Other models use a copper band that completely encircles the operator's head. Both versions work equally well. Some have even been constructed using strands of copper wire wrapped around the crystal several times and then wrapped around the operator's head. They all work.

Like the other crystal tools, a number of ornately decorated or modified models have been constructed by creative individuals who wanted to embellish a personal headband with their ideas.

The solid silver headband is very popular. It makes this crystal device a beautiful jewelry item that is suitable for many occasions. Silversmiths are also able to mount the crystal and silver disk with silver or silver solder so that it becomes a very sturdy one-piece unit, as opposed to a three-piece unit as originally designed.

Silver disks, crystals, healing stones and gemstones have been mounted on both copper and silver bands. Sometimes only two or three stones, or at times up to a dozen, are equally spaced completely around the headband.

Quartz crystals—amethyst, smoky quartz and rose quartz— are among the most popular additions to headbands. Stones such as lapis, jade, agate, citrine, turquoise and malachite have become quite popular on headbands, since most members of the mineral kingdom work well together in a balanced field of harmonious energy.

Crystal headbands were originally used for thought transmission communication in both past and present ages. Individual awareness and growth through meditation is also stimulated through the use of headbands.

Wherever crystals are used, healing with energy balancing usually occurs. For this reason the crystal headbands are now becoming popular tools of healing. They are often used in conjunction with energy rods, other crystals and even black box type radionic healing machines.

The standard headband uses a one-inch wide copper strip with a 1½-inch diameter silver disk in combination with a ½- to 1½-inch single termination quartz crystal. Double termination crystals also work very well on headbands. Many silver shapes, such as crosses, triangles and pyramid forms, work equally well. Copper bands, both wider and thinner than one inch, have proven adequate for headband construction. The instant bonding glues used do not seem to interfere with the energy operation of headbands in any way. Some people prefer to mount the crystal and silver by bending and shaping the copper band to hold them without the use of glue or solder. This works well if it can be done so that the crystal and silver piece do not fall out.

9. *Crystal communicator/generator variations and modifications.*

A number of questions have been asked about the construction of the large crystal communicator, which is simply a large crystal put in a copper cup that is usually placed on a brass plate in the center of a healing circle. Should the crystal slide all the way into the copper cup so that it touches the bottom? No, the crystal does not need to touch the bottom of the cup. It should fit tightly enough to stay in position with the tip pointing straight up. The space between the crystal and the bottom of the copper cup can vary with no effect on performance or operation of this crystal machine. Crystals in this device have been fitted to the cup with copper tape, copper mesh/screen and even silicone caulking with no adverse effects. Copper cups have been mounted to the copper plates or disks with both solder and glue. On many occasions the cups have not been attached to the plate at all. They merely sit in the center so that the crystal cup can be taken off and set elsewhere when the device is not in use. The size of the plate or disk seems to make little difference. There are many sizes in use today.

Do other materials improve the performance of this crystal tool? No, but a wide variety of materials can be substituted for part or all of this device. Copper has been the most popular material so far, but brass plates and cups are also in use. Silver plates and cups are also quite common. Bronze is another good material. Gold is a good material but is not often used because of the high price involved. Various combinations of these materials are frequently used together, such as a copper cup on a brass or silver plate, or a silver cup and a copper plate. All combinations seem to work well with no material being better than another.

Waves of energy in color and heat have been manifested with this device. This has usually been because of the operator, not the materials.

10. *Crystal shields—cluster, single and double terminated.*
    Like other crystals, the size of a crystal cluster depends on your choice. A three- to four-inch diameter cluster with crystals up to an inch in length is adequate for a garden crystal arrangement. This size is still

easily portable after being set on white quartz rocks, since many people set their garden crystal clusters inside the house during the winter months.

Larger clusters are frequently set inside the home for beneficial energy fields. The larger clusters sometimes radiate a wider field of energy and are used as artistic decorator pieces. The price of the clusters is usually the determining factor. The larger pieces do not create a stronger force field (that's determined by the person programming them), just a force field or shield with a wider area of energy inside it.

Clusters of clear quartz crystals of any size tend to radiate an intense energy field by themselves. A white quartz rock base extends this energy field so that it's not quite as intense. There are many other ways to mellow out a clear quartz crystal field without decreasing the strength. One of the most common ways is to intersperse amethyst crystals and amethyst clusters around the clear crystals in the house. Another way is to place rose or pink quartz rocks near or underneath the clear clusters, especially if an unconditionally loving energy field is desired. Blue and green quartz rocks such as adventurine also combine well to produce balanced energy fields. The color combinations of quartz crystals and quartz rocks cover a wide spectrum of energy combinations. It's best to experiment until you find one that feels right for you.

Clear, cloudy and milky quartz crystals radiate their own frequencies of energy. Black or smoky quartz crystals and rocks add another dimension to this energy, as do purple or amethyst rocks and crystals. Pink or rose quartz crystals or rocks (rose quartz crystals and clusters are rather expensive) also bring about an energy balance. Yellow or brown citrine quartz crystals and clusters bring in another vibration of energy.

With the blue and green quartz rocks, an unlimited number of degrees of energy combinations are possible for arranging a balanced energy field or shield.

Quite often pink, blue and green quartz rocks are sawed into quarter-inch thick slices or plates and used as a base to set other crystals or clusters on. Slices of clear, milky and cloudy quartz crystals have also been used, although it's good to ask a complete crystal if it wants to be cut up for this purpose. A slab or rock base can change energy and be decorative, but a crystal cluster can be placed directly on the ground, floor or table.

Wherever there is a quartz crystal, there is an interaction and radiation of energy. At one time people thought that quartz crystals below a half inch in diameter were much less powerful and should not be used. Crystals smaller than this have since been used in the small copper tubes set in the four directions of a garden. These small crystals with both covered (leather wrapped) and uncovered copper rods have worked just as well as larger crystals. Smaller crystals have also performed well in pocket- and purse-size energy rods. Even tiny crystals (⅛" diameter and smaller) have been used in miniature energy rods and jewelry.

Double termination crystals have been in use as personal energy field/shield projectors for quite some time. The same size illusion was involved here too. Some people thought any double termination crystal smaller than an inch or two in length wouldn't work as a personal energy shield, so of course the crystals didn't work. Now it's common for tiny double termination crystals (less than ½" in length) to be programmed and carried as individual energy shields. All quartz crystals are of the same subatomic structure created by the Earth Mother. They are all connected to the universal web of energy by their nature.

Likewise, single termination crystals of all sizes have been found to work well as personal energy shields, although many people report that the double termination crystals seem to radiate a more well-rounded and balanced energy field.

11. *Weather, nature and crystals.*

Quartz crystals and weather conditions are electromagnetic in nature, so an interrelationship of energy fields has already been established for use according to our balanced understanding.

Clouds are a good example of levitation (the term *antigravity* doesn't quite fit). Tons of water vapor float through the atmosphere with ease because of a balance of positive and negative ions. Mother Nature provides amazing examples of the types of conditions and phenomena we wish to understand and duplicate. The techniques used to float clouds and float huge stones to build pyramids and other structures in ancient times may prove to be no different at all. The same type of example can be found in the running water of streams and rivers, thunderstorms and lightning, and quartz crystals. These all produce negative ions to balance with the positive ions. Crystal workers soon learn to look to Mother Nature, humankind's greatest teacher, for examples of energy changes she uses to maintain a balance of creativity in nurturing her life forms.

Lightning above the Earth and quartz crystals below the Earth produce the electromagnetic interactions that foster all life, which is electromagnetic by nature. When an eagle soars upon the winds, both the wind and the eagle are one with the electromagnetic energy spectrum.

The Earth Mother herself is a giant electromagnetic being, turning like an electric motor or generator on her axis. Her underground movements (earthquakes and volcanoes) are electromagnetic in nature. Piezoelectric crystals and minerals, and magnetic rocks such as lodestone and magnetite all function within her electrical system. The electromagnetic mineral kingdom lives in balance with her other electromagnetic beings: plants, birds, fish, animals and people. Human beings using crystals are energy generators as well. The Earth lives in electromagnetic balance with other planets, the Moon, asteroids, the Sun and other stars of the larger being—the electromagnetic Universe of flowing interacting energy.

Solar storms and earth storms in the sea of universal electromagnetic energy are different only in intensity and type of energy. The process is the same, even carried on out into intergalactic storms in the Universal Star Sea. The nature of weather is the same in any area, electromagnetic within the subatomic realm.

Human beings as electrical connections have a great influence on the Earth Mother's weather, consciously or unconsciously. In this area all is one and intimately connected by the Universal Energy. Consciously being at one with the storm beings can be as much fun as being at one with the crystal beings of the mineral world. The use of crystals for the conscious influence of the weather is a practice dating back to the beginning of humankind.

One of the easiest practices in weather modification still in use involves using a crystal rod or a crystal by itself. When clouds and rain or snow are needed for an area of the Earth Mother, use a process of balancing and healing the Earth's body and aura as you would for a person, plant or animal. Like most crystal practices, visualizing or picturing the effect desired in the mind is the beginning. Being one with it follows. In this case, see the clouds forming in the blue sky. Visualizing the clouds brings the particles, electrons, ions and water droplets together to form giant "cells in the sky," along with their thunder and lightning. With the appropriate pictures in mind, the intense feeling of love and at-oneness with the crystal, Earth Mother and self amplifies the healing manifestation. The crystal being and the Earth being both want to work with you in this area—promoting life and growth—and that's what the Earth Mother's nurturing is all about anyway, whether we decide to be in harmony with it or not.

We are learning to be friends with the Earth Mother's crystal and mineral beings, her plant and animal beings and maybe her other human beings. Well, sometimes, anyway. If we want to influence weather, it's a practical idea to start feeling a kinship with the Earth's weather beings. Seeing or feeling them as friends is a great way to establish this relationship. Friendly beings won't hurt us, so there's nothing to fear. It may be a bit disconcerting to try at-oneness and unconditional love with a hurricane or a tornado, so try someone easier at first. Cloud beings are nice. Thunder and lightning beings are always willing to put on a show while trying to get our attention. There's also the wind spirits, who can be gentle or strong, warm or cold. In the summer there's the little whirlwinds who like to play cute tricks, even if it gets dust in our eyes. Maybe that's why we sometimes call them little dust devils. Far above in the upper atmosphere there's the giant, fast moving wind circling the Earth Mother.

There are also other weather beings we can get to

know. For instance, Aurora Borealis at the poles, and earthquakes, who are always expressing themselves and trying to shake us up.

It should come as no great surprise by now that the reason it is so easy to influence the Earth's weather is that we are already doing so, though not always in the conscious ways that we like. Humankind's mass consciousness of thoughts and emotions permeates the Earth Mother's aura and her geomagnetic field. Her weather beings are born, grow, change and move within her aura and the same geomagnetic field. The difference is that mass consciousness is unconscious, undirected and unfocused in its influence on weather energy patterns.

Since we are already connected to and are part of the Earth's electromagnetic field, it is a relatively simple practice to focus our thoughts and emotions (with a feeling of unconditional love, I hope) on projecting the specific weather effects we need around the Earth for balance and healing.

As individuals, modifying our weather patterns by projecting thoughts with the help of our crystal energy friends is an effective way of increasing energy for our purposes. Throughout human history on our planet, individuals, as friends of the Earth, have used quartz crystals for doing this. Druids, Atlanteans, Egyptians, witches, magicians, scientists and medicine people have been doing this for a long time. One person or a group of people in a circle around a crystal can not only form clouds but also call upon the wind spirit beings to come and manifest themselves. In fact with a crystal, one can call upon any kind of weather being. This is not so much a power (although people like to call it that) as it is a cooperative relationship between electric beings who are part of the same overall electromagnetic field of a larger being.

Learning to feel at one with the beings of Mother Nature is more a lifestyle than a learning of knowledge. Thinking and feeling are more important than following anyone else's technique in this area. There are as many ways to do it as there are individual persons. There is no one "right way," but many ways that all work. This is definitely not a procedure of connecting part A to piece B or following steps 1, 2, 3, and 4. Our so-called modern society uses procedures like that in industry and business, but these are artificial forms of thinking that do not apply to a personal relationship with the Earth Mother and her friendly beings. In this area you are your own best guide.

12. *Why do authors of crystal books have contradictory statements about crystal usage?*

Crystals and human beings are unique individuals. Some of each are similar, but no two are exactly alike. Crystal beings are very sensitive in response to human beings. Crystals will react to exactly the way we think and feel, in varying degrees, on all levels. Our self-created world responds the same way. While it's easy for two people to elicit the same reaction from a crystal, or crystals, it's just as easy to get two different and even opposite reactions from them.

13. *What is the difference between personal and impersonal energy?*

The energy of the Universe is, in essence, all the same. It appears different when minds form and direct it to new purposes for their own creations. Before this is done, the energy is impersonal and undifferentiated. Afterwards it can become personal, or it can be focused in a way that does not personalize it.

9 Crystals—The Other Side of the Coin

"New Age people sometimes pretend that they never get the blues, but sometimes they do."

What do we do when crystals appear not to work, or appear to work in what some would consider a negative fashion?

Remember that crystals are a reflection of ourselves. Crystals and crystal elemental energy respond to our thoughts and emotions. Look at yourself, outside and inside, to determine what you are doing, and you'll be able to tell what the crystals are doing with you.

Quartz crystal energy beings respond to the finest subtleties and nuances of our mental, emotional and spiritual consciousness or awareness. They react to our aura of energy, our total bioelectromagnetic energy field. They want to do what we are doing and be what we are being, right now, no matter what that is.

When crystals appear not to do anything for some people (this applies to crystal tools too), it usually means that the person doesn't really think, believe or feel that the crystals are conscious energy beings. It's relatively easy to relate to a being of the plant or animal kingdom, but it's sometimes difficult for people to relate in the same way to a being of the mineral kingdom. This usually reflects a person's ability to relate to the Earth Mother as a conscious being and the Sky Father (the Universe or Great Spirit) as an even larger being. If this is the case, we should relax and be kind to and accepting of ourselves. The crystal beings are going to do what we are doing whether we are conscious of it or not.

Working with crystals, or just having them sit around the house, car or office, does two things simultaneously. It speeds up our evolution, awareness and personal growth, and it does the same thing for elemental crystal beings.

Crystals are going to amplify and manifest changes and new growth patterns for the evolution of our inner selves. This is often disconcerting and disturbing if our minds or everyday conscious awareness is not keeping up with this process. In everyday events this can frequently mean a change of mates, change of homes, change of geographical location or changes in career that stimulate our talents and personal growth. With crystals there is no resting on our laurels; if we don't move toward growth, they and our inner spirit will move us. This process can be interpreted negatively as a loss, or it can be accepted as a gain, depending on the choice of our own emotional-mental state of mind awareness.

Once this process is started in motion by our choice to grow and work with crystals, it is advisable to accept the changes as gracefully and good-naturedly as possible, since our inner selves, the spirit that is us, has already chosen what's best for us. The Universe is providing what we need and what we choose at this point. Often in crystal work, energy frequency changes happen so fast that they can be interpreted as bad. Further reflection and introspection usually shows that this is not the case at all. Nonetheless, the fast changes frequently prove to be traumatic.

One of the most common cases of Crystal Karma (cause and effect) is the cold or flu that follows an "out of balance" emotional outburst of anger, hostility or depression. This usually means that the body is rejecting the negativity to rebalance itself.

Crystals will amplify everything that a person might be doing, including the mental and emotional moods and thoughts that seek expression or manifestation in the outer world. This is why it's so important to know ourselves. Any type of negative emotion such as fear, anger, depression or jealousy will be amplified, as well as positives such as love, peace, kindness and understanding. This is not necessarily bad. Sometimes it is important for us to become painfully aware of our feelings so that we can deal with them and move ahead on our life's path.

The Universal Energy that flows through crystals and people is impersonal. It does not judge how or why something is being created. It responds and manifests exactly as the mind of the human creator thinks or visualizes. The use of crystals speeds up the process of cause and effect, sometimes to the point of almost "instant karma," which helps crystal people speed up their own self-development and understanding of how the energy works.

As we study crystals, even down to subatomic particle patterns of Universal Energy, we are seeing more and more reflections of the energy beings that show us ourselves. Whether it's the study of the Universe or the study of quartz crystals, it is mainly the study of self. The patterns and relationships of energy involved with our own actions and reactions show us what we are—as integrated, moving parts of the One Universal Energy. We cannot turn the energy on or off, but we can guide and channel its expression, direction and manifestation. It is an individual choice and responsibility. What we see in our mind (visualize) is what is created and projected. What we are is what we get. Our beings work energy in whatever way our minds and higher or inner selves determine.

Anyone who works with crystals will have to face self and parts of self time and time again—not only those aspects of self that are pleasing but also the more disturbing aspects of self. This process will continue until self-love and respect are accepted. Harsh judgment and self-criticism are not appropriate ways for a crystal person to deal with self, since these will be amplified by the crystals.

This also applies when crystals or crystal rods don't do anything at all. It is the self inside the operator that determines—by inner beliefs, feeling and thoughts— whether or not the Universal Energy of the crystal is flowing in a balanced fashion. The operator's thoughts and feelings, especially deep-seated feelings, affect the crystal beings who affect the amplification of energy or lack of flow.

Crystals augment, amplify and speed up a process that is already in motion. This process is the programming and creation of our own lives and circumstances. These events or situations are reflected by our minds. Mind/self creates all, and crystals go with what we are already doing. Good thoughts and emotions are a must for conscious self-creators to avoid negative feedback and increase the positive.

Crystals guide us to the mind of the creator, the mind of our higher inner self . . . ALL THAT IS. It is all Mind. This includes everything from channeling to meeting extraterrestrials, shopping at the grocery store, making love, watching an eagle soar across the sky or seeing the Moon rise full into the night above the Earth. From washing our faces to astral travel to another planet, it is all Mind, the Mind of One in motion and relationship to itself.

Crystals and crystal books are only guides and helpers in the realization of self. Living, knowing and being from our own conscious experience is what all the masters, teachers and sacred books have been saying for thousands of years. As we go towards the 21st century, we are our only guides.

KRYSTAL KARMA

Karma exists, like everything else, because we think it does. We sometimes think it's instant. Sometimes we think it's lifetime to lifetime, year to year, or decade to decade. It can be be all of these things or none, depending on what we think at a given time. It may exist or it may not, but the Universe moves energy to provide a balance in creation regardless of what we believe.

We tend to think everything and everybody else thinks the same way we do, which is not necessarily so. The Universe, elementals and plants do not think like we do. We are all a part of the same whole. To understand, we need to think, sense and feel as they do.

Their job is to be and to do—not to be inhibited in being and doing by thinking, worrying or being concerned about cause and effect (karma). While we're busy self-dividing ourselves by thought and belief, the rest of creation is busy just being, selflessly and unconditionally. When we learn to do that, we're expressing unconditional love. We are being in balance.

When we are in balance, karma does not exist. When we are not in balance, the Universe may move energy to balance us. We might call it good or bad karma, but it's just balance. Working with crystals moves energy very quickly to bring about this balance.

10 The Crystal Channel

"All music, song and dance is, by its nature, channeled."

Channeling is using the energy information lines that connect and interrelate all things and beings in the Universe. It can be done consciously or unconsciously. What we commonly refer to as channeling is usually of the conscious variety.

The crystal augments and amplifies this natural, preexisting matrix of energy-based data transmission and reception. Crystals are the radios and televisions of the Universe and the Earth Mother's planetary computer. Crystals function as memory chips, capacitors, transducers, amplifiers, transmitters and receivers. Quartz crystals also act as transformers on the invisible lines of force or power of the Universal Source.

Energy is produced at the universal power station and transmitted through the lines of force to numerous substations, transformers and outlets. This energy is then monitored and recorded by the computer-like ganglion and memory banks at the Source's power station. This is the energy that the Universal Intelligence produces and transmits for the creation and recreation of ourselves and all things in existence. People and crystals function as substations, transformers and outlets for the Universal Energy to keep creating an ever-expanding Universe. This process is just like wiring in new outlets in an electrical system to tap into the main power lines. These new outlets can then be used to transmit energy to new areas, providing power for new creations.

It is not, and never has been, necessary for people or crystals to try to transmit power back to the Source. The power from the universal power station is an unlimited supply. It flows, like electricity, from the higher to the lower, ever outward through people, crystals and other created forms. These forms are always connected to and monitored by the Universal Source of Awareness. This is true regardless of the degree of awareness the created forms or circuits have of this process at any given time. The flow of energy is naturally outward to connect and form new creations so that the Source of the Universe can continue its growth.

Attempts by circuits or outlets along these invisible energy lines to transmit energy back to the source are going against the flow of Universal Power. This causes shorts or opens in the power lines, blocking or interrupting the smooth flow of energy. These usually get repaired after some disruption of service. Some parts are even replaced completely. The flow of energy outward from the Source and on through the crystal people always seeks to create a harmoniously balanced energy path to its new creations.

Positive and negative balance of polarities plays a major part in this flow of energy. Like the terminals of a battery or the poles of a magnet, both are necessary for the creative energy path. This balance of male and female, or yin and yang, produces a harmonious energy field that radiates as a circle or sphere of energy. The Universal Energy creates new forms and remains connected to the new creations. It then continues to power the new forms it has created.

In human experience on planet Earth, song, dance and art are channeled. They always have been, we just haven't used that term. There are many other experiences of the life process that involve the channeling of energy and information. A channel or medium of expression has always been required for Universal Energy (Spirit) to manifest the physical reality we see. This is just Universal Energy with form contained within an electromagnetic field. The nature of the Universe is channeled energy.

The Creator makes all of creation come about by channeling energy through an infinite variety of mediums. This includes everything from rocks, crystals, fish, birds, animals, people, trees, stars, planets and seeds to God knows what. Some people like to make channeling mysterious, a term of special significance. It is special, significant and sacred because it's everywhere and everything, but it is not particularly mysterious. An inspirational work such as the Bible is channeled, but so is the idea for an electric can opener, a television, a disc brake and a political doctrine. If you exist, you're channeling energy in one form or another. It's all that exists. It's all that is. That's the way it works.

11   Crystal Light Rods

"Crystals, like people, sometimes get excited."

The Crystal Light Rod is the basic power rod with a penlight addition. It is one of the more complex crystal rod constructions, but it is also one of the most powerful and entertaining rods to use. It is a rod well worth constructing.

The subatomic energy structure within a quartz crystal gets excited when it's exposed to light and the small amount of heat that is emitted by a penlight bulb. At this point the elemental energy being inside the crystal starts dancing. The crystal being is also responding to the biomagnetic aura of the crystal rod operator as the energy is directed from the hand to the penlight and crystal.

The light provides an opportunity to see a wide variety of scenes, pictures, recordings of history on Earth and something of ourselves. I mean really looking at a crystal from all angles with our physical sight. We sometimes spend so much effort in feeling or sensing psychically that it's an enlightening experience to examine the crystal world using more of our physical perception. There is a lot to be seen in the crystal kingdom that is in plain sight and not hidden at all.

Like other crystal devices and experiments, the information about crystal light rods is meant to be a guideline or a starting point. Any type of flashlight will light up a crystal. If an exact type is not easily obtainable, use one that is. There are many models of penlights on the market, but larger lights will still do the most important thing: lighting up a crystal so that we can see and learn.

The instructions in my book *Crystal Power* explain power rod construction in more detail. The two main differences in the crystal light rod are the use of copper mesh screen or copper tape for mounting the crystal securely and the penlight installation. The shape and depth of the quartz crystal in the mounting change slightly for each rod. The length varies according to the mounting of the copper coupler (lined with foil tape) as a bulb guard and reflector. It's a good practice to cut the main copper pipe longer than the approximate six inches. This allows the pipe to be cut shorter as the penlight is fitted so that the push button switch will work properly. The major components of the light rod should be built in separate units.

CRYSTAL LIGHT ROD—MODEL 1

Construction

1. The crystal should be glued (instant bonding glue) inside the reducer, using ¾-inch wide strips of copper mesh, tape or leather wrapped around the crystal as an inside shim.
2. The ½-inch copper coupler to be used for a light bulb guard is lined with shiny foil tape inside and glued to the penlight.
3. The ¾-inch copper pipe should be cut an inch or two longer than the six inches so that it can be cut down to exactly fit the penlight after the crystal mount-reducer is glued on one end of the pipe.

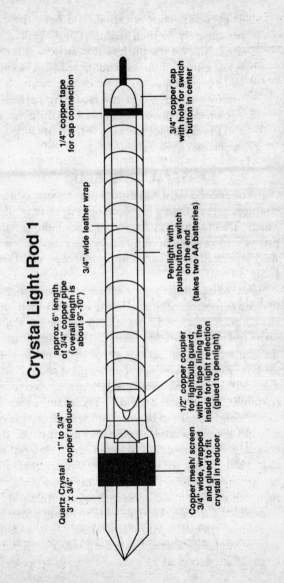

Crystal Light Rod 1

1/4" copper tape for cap connection

3/4" copper cap with hole for switch button in center

3/4" wide leather wrap

Penlight with pushbutton switch on the end (takes two AA batteries)

approx. 6" length of 3/4" copper pipe (overall length is about 9"-10")

1/2" copper coupler for lightbulb guard, with foil tape lining the inside for light reflection (glued to penlight)

1" to 3/4" copper reducer

Quartz Crystal 3" x 3/4"

Copper mesh/ screen 3/4" wide, wrapped and glued to fit crystal in reducer

4. The ¾-inch copper cap should have the approximately ¼-inch diameter hole drilled in the center for the push button switch. This cap is not glued on the end but taped with ¼-inch wide copper tape so that it can be taken off to remove the penlight for changing batteries. (Colored filters can be put between the penlight and the crystal for working with colors through the crystal.)

CRYSTAL LIGHT ROD 2

The second light rod model uses several copper couplers rather than one piece of copper pipe. It is much easier to build if you can find a penlight with the push button switch on the end. Some grocery, hardware and drug stores carry this model of penlight and some do not.

After acquiring the penlight it's a simple matter to remove the pocket clip and slide on the ½-inch copper couplings. Leave the switch cap exposed so that it turns freely for changing batteries and bulbs. Four of the copper couplings can be glued to the penlight as they are fitted. The fifth copper coupling should have the quartz crystal mounted in it before it's glued to the flashlight. The crystal should be less than ½ inch in diameter so that it can be wrapped with reflective tin foil and copper screen or tape and glued inside the coupling. This should all be fitted and tested on the penlight before glue is applied so that adjustments can be made easily. The quartz crystal should be relatively clear so that it lights up brightly. It should be fitted so that it doesn't touch the bulb or put pressure on it causing a malfunction. The crystal can be as long as you want. The average size used is 1½" to 3" so a large area of crystal is exposed to light up well.

Crystal Light Rod 2

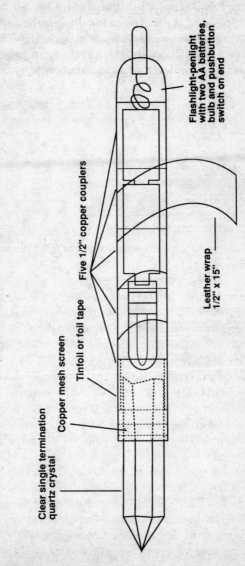

Flashlight-penlight with two AA batteries, bulb and pushbutton switch on end

Five 1/2" copper couplers

Leather wrap 1/2" x 15"

Tinfoil or foil tape

Copper mesh screen

Clear single termination quartz crystal

After this is assembled, the strip of leather can be wrapped and glued in place to complete the unit. This makes a smaller, more convenient pocket light rod for easy carrying. These also provide the fun of being able to see into the depth of the quartz crystal.

12 Crystal Wands, Crystal Hands and the Ankh Crystallos

"Ki or Chi is the essence of the Universe."

The crystal hands and crystal wands were manifested for use in self-development practices. They help us experience the extension of the energy of self into the larger world—the experience of being one with the energy of the planet and Universe. We are then able to tune into the higher, all-encompassing self.

The experience of feeling the Earth's life energy flowing up through the soles of the feet is combined with feeling the energy pouring downward from the Universe through the top of the head. These two flows of energy follow a path outward through the arms and hands. The flow continues through the hand and wands and is projected outward from the focal points of the quartz crystals.

This is a process of learning by doing. The experience itself is much more than a written description can explain.

The crystal hands and the crystal wands lend themselves to use in a wide variety of martial arts forms. Using the Chi energy of Tai Chi Chuan, the Ki energy of Aikido or any of the other terms you prefer from the various practices, you are still using the same Universal Energy of healing and quartz crystals.

THE CRYSTAL HANDS

The use of the crystal hands applies to many areas and techniques of these martial arts forms. Like all crystal work, this is an individual choice according to "feeling." Most practitioners of the arts are more in tune with the Universal Energy than they give themselves credit for or accept. While most martial arts are, by their nature, in harmony with the Earth Mother, some practices lend themselves especially to the use of the crystal hands. These tools can easily be applied to the animal and bird forms used in some techniques. It is a time of growth, not of retreat to the traditional practices of an earlier time. Now is the time to expand the growth of the tradition to come. This insures peace and harmony, both inner and outer, providing the peace and balance for the future. The moving energy of our future is created now on the Earth Mother planet. Now is the only time anything can be done, regardless of whether it is of a positive or a negative impact. The crystal hands manifest positive and negative as a balance of the male/female energy.

Materials and Construction

These crystal tools are usually constructed in pairs. Each one uses three ½-inch diameter copper couplings and four ½-inch diameter copper 45-degree angle elbows to form the "U" shape. The couplings and the elbows are fitted together using six ¾-inch lengths of ½-inch copper pipe. Instant bonding glue is used to secure the joints. All joints should be fitted

Crystal Hands

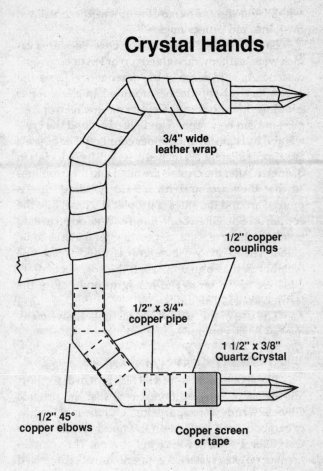

3/4" wide
leather wrap

1/2" copper
couplings

1/2" x 3/4"
copper pipe

1 1/2" x 3/8"
Quartz Crystal

1/2" 45°
copper elbows

Copper screen
or tape

without glue first, to be sure the unit will fit securely at the joints and proper angles.

Each U-shaped hand can be covered with a ¾-inch wide leather wrap (glued on) or left uncovered if desired. As with some of the other crystal tools, the quartz crystal should be mounted in the copper coupling first as one unit. Copper mesh screen or copper tape can be wrapped and glued around the crystals and fitted inside the copper coupling. The crystals are approximately 1½ inches in length by ⅜ inches in diameter. After the crystals are fitted into the couplings so that they are straight, instant bonding glue is poured around the sides, a droplet at a time, into the copper screen. Often both liquid and quick gel instant bonding glue are used, depending on the area to be glued. The U-shaped handgrip is fitted and glued together first as one unit. Then the crystal coupling ends are glued on to the handgrip unit before the leather wrap is glued on.

The use of this pair of crystal tools allows many martial arts techniques to be practiced.

THE CRYSTAL WANDS

The crystal wands are a bit different in that little is known about the tradition except that the original Chinese wands were approximately four-foot lengths of bamboo—not staff length and not short like the Tai Chi Ruler, but somewhere in between. The complement of quartz crystals in copper reducers connected by the spirals of copper tape amplifies the crystal energy. Single or double termination quartz crystals can be used. This provides a powerful energy manifestation. Like the crystal hands, your judgment as to how to use the wand is the ultimate guide. You are the key.

Crystal Wands

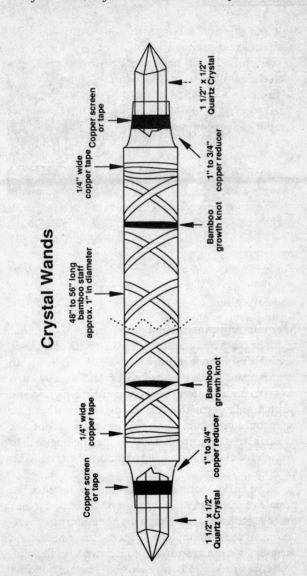

1 1/2" x 1/2" Quartz Crystal

Copper screen or tape

1" to 3/4" copper reducer

1/4" wide copper tape

Bamboo growth knot

48" to 56" long bamboo staff approx. 1" in diameter

1/4" wide copper tape

Bamboo growth knot

Copper screen or tape

1" to 3/4" copper reducer

1 1/2" x 1/2" Quartz Crystal

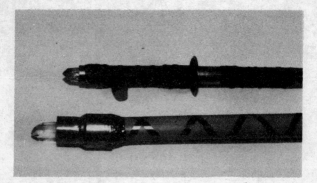

Materials and construction

The main body of the wand is a length of bamboo (available in most import stores). We look for an approximate diameter of one inch and usually cut a six-foot length to about 48 inches; say between 44 and 56 inches. The growth knots will determine where the cut should be made. Most cuts are made about two inches above the growth knots so that the one-inch to ¾-inch reducers can be used to mount the crystals on each end.

The Earth Mother does not always instruct her people of the plant kingdom to grow bamboo to our exact specifications. We go with her energy manifestations. If the bamboo end is more than one inch in diameter, we file, rasp and sand it down to fit the one-inch copper reducer before we glue (instant bonding glue) the reducer with the crystal mounted on it to the end. About 30 feet of ¼-inch wide copper tape is wrapped in crossing spirals along the entire length of the bamboo before the reducers with crystals are mounted. The quartz crystals, approximately 1½ inches long by ½ inches in diameter, are mounted in the copper reducers using copper mesh screen or copper tape wrap as shims. The wrapped part of the crystal is soaked with instant bonding glue (a drop at a time) after it is inserted into the ¾-inch end of the reducer. The bamboo with the copper spiral wrap is built as one unit. The crystal fitted to the copper reducer is also built as one unit. Then the crystal reducer is fitted and glued to each end of bamboo wand. Do not hesitate to modify or change anything to suit your preference. You are the only judge of what is right for you.

An excellent book for reference is *Aikido and the New Warrior* by Richard Heckler, available from North Atlantic Books, 2320 Blake Street, Berkeley, CA 94704.

THE ANKH CRYSTALLOS

The Ankh Crystallos is familiar to anyone who knows it as the Egyptian symbol of eternal life. The study of ancient civilizations reveals this as an archetype (symbol in our genetic or mass consciousness) that activates a deeply emotional feeling. With a double-terminated quartz crystal in the top loop of the ankh, we have another extremely alive power tool for health and life. The dimensions of this crystal cross are 10 to 11 inches tall by 5½ to 6 inches wide on the cross piece. The healers of Egypt acquired knowledge of this tool from Atlantis when it was a colony. Later, ankh-bearing Atlanteans found refuge in Egypt after the last island of Atlantis (Poseidon) sank beneath the ocean. The Atlanteans acquired the knowledge off-world from a civilization in the Pleiades. A symbol of the eternal life force is only natural for people attuned to the one Source.

The crystal ankh is a powerful balancing and healing tool, radiating the energy of peace and long life. This is very important on Earth right now, since peace makes long life possible. Peace and eternal life also require the constant conscious expression of joy and happiness, so it is important to feel these emotions while using it.

Its uses include healing, blessing, and meditation, either individually or in groups. This crystal tool is active at all times after it is constructed, owing to its pattern, shape and form combined with the double termination quartz crystal. During outdoor circles or ceremonies the ankh can be set upright in the ground for a harmonious Earth contact. It is especially powerful for radiating light energy to help human beings maintain balance. This can help us raise our consciousness in order to tune into the Creator for Universal Energy.

This object is quite compatible with most religious practices, since our modern religions descended from the Atlantean and Egyptian traditions. Larger versions of the crystal ankh are becoming quite popular along with even smaller jewelry-size creations set in silver instead of copper. Size and color are determined by the intuition of the person who is going to be using the Ankh Crystallos. This is a very peaceful reinvention. As usual, your intuition is the best guide for using this.

The looped cross, as a symbol of life, is a radiator of the energy of peace, love, trust, health and abundance. The loop with the cross gives us an example of

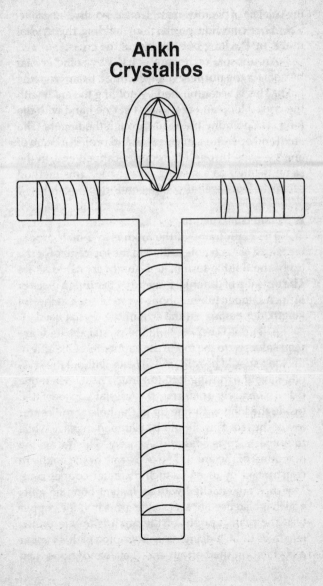

Ankh
Crystallos

the balance of polarity: male/female, positive/negative. The most common position for holding this crystal tool is by the long bottom arm of the cross.

An unusual technique is used by some crystal healers for the purpose of projecting a beam from the ankh. This is accomplished by holding the ankh with the crystal loop and cross arms in one hand with the long arm pointing outward through the fingers. The ankh and operator can visualize and project a beam of energy, even through the copper-capped end, in the same manner as a healing power rod. This method seems to work well if you're comfortable with it.

Parts and construction

The main frame of the ankh is a ½-inch copper tee with a ⅜-inch hole drilled in the top center for the tip of the double-terminated quartz crystal to sit in. The top loop of the ankh is made by bending a piece of ¼-inch copper tubing about three to four inches in length, depending on the size of the crystal used.

After this is bent to hold the crystal, the ends are then soldered to the top of the copper tee. One side of the loop should be soldered in place without the crystal to avoid exposing it to too much heat. When one side is securely soldered, the crystal can be fitted inside the loop with one tip in the hole at the center top of the tee. This should be clamped in place while the other side is soldered securely. This forms the main unit of the ankh. The two arms of the ankh are constructed by using ½-inch diameter copper pipe. The caps are attached with an instant bonding glue, which is also used to secure the arms into the copper tee. The main upright of the ankh is an eight-inch length of ½-inch diameter copper pipe with a copper cap glued on the bottom end. This handgrip is then

Ankh Crystallos

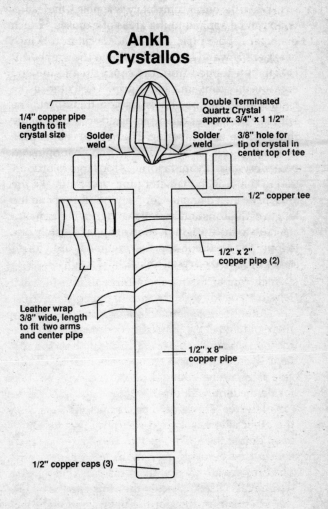

1/4" copper pipe length to fit crystal size

Double Terminated Quartz Crystal approx. 3/4" x 1 1/2"

Solder weld

Solder weld

3/8" hole for tip of crystal in center top of tee

1/2" copper tee

1/2" x 2" copper pipe (2)

Leather wrap 3/8" wide, length to fit two arms and center pipe

1/2" x 8" copper pipe

1/2" copper caps (3)

glued into the bottom opening of the copper tee.

When the unit is completely assembled, the leather wrap can be applied to the areas of exposed ½-inch diameter copper pipe. The leather is cut into ⅜-inch or wider strips and glued to the pipe as it is wrapped. It is usually wrapped from the copper tee to the end caps on the arms and hand grip. The color of the leather wrap can be chosen as you think best. The width of the leather can be adjusted according to the thickness for easy covering. The ½-inch copper pipe is adequate for several sizes of double-terminated quartz crystals. If your favorite is too large in proportion to the ½-inch diameter pipe, you can make the ankh of ¾-inch diameter copper pipe and expand the length of the arms and upright handgrip. The arms are at a ratio to the upright portion of approximately one to four. The same construction method is used for all stages of any size crystal ankh.

13 Crystal Dowsing Tools, Dark Crystals and Crystals of Imperfect Perfection

"I think Crystal Power *started when I found out I was a plumber in a previous lifetime."*

Instructions for making crystal dowsing tools is included here for the patient people who have been asking what I can provide in the area of dowsing that relates to the crystal world. While I have been using dowsing rods and pendulums for many years, there are two tools that stand out as exceptional in my experience. The crystal dowsing rods were developed by adapting the power rod technology to standard dowsing rods with the intention of improving accuracy and response for the dowser. These have worked for me, and I hope you can use them with as much success.

CRYSTAL DOWSING PENDULUM
The crystal dowsing pendulum literally chose me and told me that it was to be used for that purpose. It took me awhile to catch on, so the crystals and crystal beings involved used the direct action approach. This came as quite a surprise to me, but they did get the message across over a period of weeks. Let me explain how this came about.

The pendulum was originally a pendant made by one of my friends at the mineral shop. It is a unique design: a double-terminated quartz crystal is held horizontally by a band of silver in the center, and an amethyst crystal (single-terminated) mounted in silver hangs from the center band on the quartz crystal. I couldn't put it down when I first picked it up to look at it. I should have guessed something was up at that point. I acquired the pendant and attached it to a silver chain to wear as a necklace. It was beautiful, but it would not hang right when I wore it. It kept getting knotted up and twisted in the chain. I thought I solved the problem by switching the pendant to a gold chain instead. This didn't help. Over a dozen times a day the chain would come unhooked and the crystals would fall down inside my shirt.

After a couple of weeks I finally got the message. This was not a pendant or a necklace. As I was looking at it one day, the pendant slid down the chain and caught perfectly in the hook on the end of the chain, making a pendulum of itself. I have used it that way since then and invariably get a very energetic response from it.

Construction and use

The crystal dowsing pendulum has two main components. The first is a double termination quartz crystal approximately 1¼ inches in length by ⅜ inches in diameter. A smaller or larger size can be used, but a much larger size might be heavy and unwieldy. The second part of this unit is a single termination amethyst crystal. The size of this one is approximately ¾ inches in length by ⅜ inches in diameter. These are attached to a ten-inch silver chain.

The silver mountings will probably have to be fitted

Crystal Dowsing Pendulum

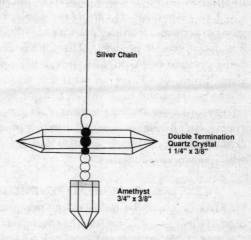

Silver Chain

Double Termination
Quartz Crystal
1 1/4" x 3/8"

Amethyst
3/4" x 3/8"

by a jeweler or silversmith after you choose your crystals. You could also use gold or silver fittings and a quartz crystal on the bottom. The combination of quartz, amethyst and silver has worked so well for me that I have not changed it.

Anyone experimenting with these probably already knows about using a pendulum for dowsing, so I will only touch on that briefly here. The operator usually asks a question that can be answered with a "yes" or a "no." The pendulum chain is then held steady in the air a few inches above a flat surface such as a table. It is often helpful to rest the elbow of the hand holding the chain on the table. When asked a question the pendulum will begin to move of its own volition. Some people prefer the clockwise motion for "yes" and the counterclockwise motion for a "no" answer. Quite a few people prefer the vertical swing for "yes," the horizontal swing for "no" and the counterclockwise motion for an "undecided" answer. Your intuition is your best guide to what's right for you.

Like all the other crystal tools available, this one is going to perform according to the talent of the operator. It is always good to be aware of the One Source when using crystals: one God, one Universal Energy, one Great Spirit, one Force, or whatever your concept might be. This will tune you in to your higher self energy for a more accurate reading. And that is you, of course, isn't it? Please remember in this process that crystals and crystal tools are also conscious beings who like working together.

CRYSTAL ARROWHEAD PENDULUM

This is one of the fastest acting pendulums I've used. It consists of a 12-inch leather thong tied around a quartz crystal arrowhead, one inch wide by three inches long. The beads shown are optional according to personal preference. The most difficult part of making this pendulum is finding a quartz crystal arrowhead. Sometimes the old ones can be found or purchased in rock shops. New ones can sometimes be acquired from enthusiasts who practice the art of arrowhead making. An arrowhead of any type will work if a quartz crystal arrowhead is not available.

SPIRAL QUARTZ PENDULUM

The simplest pendulum I've ever used is very easy to construct. This one is also the most economical when it comes to obtaining parts. The weight on the end is a quartz rock with tiny crystals or a small quartz cluster embedded in it. Most rock shops carry these.

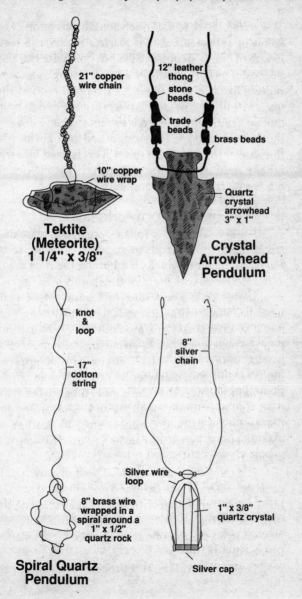

Tektite (Meteorite) 1 1/4" x 3/8"

21" copper wire chain

10" copper wire wrap

Crystal Arrowhead Pendulum

12" leather thong

stone beads

trade beads

brass beads

Quartz crystal arrowhead 3" x 1"

Spiral Quartz Pendulum

knot & loop

17" cotton string

8" brass wire wrapped in a spiral around a 1" x 1/2" quartz rock

8" silver chain

Silver wire loop

1" x 3/8" quartz crystal

Silver cap

The string used is a 17-inch length of cotton. The spiral of wire around the quartz rock is an 8-inch length of brass or copper. Silver or gold wire can also be used. The wire should be a heavy enough gauge to remain fixed in place after it's wrapped around the quartz rock. Needle-nosed pliers are needed to hold one end of the wire when it is bent to shape around the rock you choose. The string is tied to a tight loop in the wire at the top of the spiral. This is used like any other pendulum. Tektites and any other stone can be made into this type of pendulum.

CRYSTAL DOWSING RODS

The crystal dowsing rods are created by attaching small crystal power rods to standard dowsing rods. Even coat hangers will do, but I prefer the rods made of heavier metal with the plexiglass handles for smooth operation. It's a good idea to buy a set of professionally made dowsing rods to start with.

The crystal rod tips are constructed by cutting two 1⅝-inch lengths of ¼-inch diameter copper tubing. A single termination quartz crystal approximately ¼ inch in diameter by one inch in length is then mounted in each of the copper tubes in the standard way of splitting the tubes and using an instant bonding glue to hold them in. Strips of leather or colored tape ¼ inch wide can then be used to wrap the crystal rods.

The most energetic crystals I've found are a pair consisting of one right-hand and one left-hand crystal. Most crystals are either right or left, but in this case try to find some that are quite distinctly right and left. You may want to ask someone at a rock shop for assistance in selecting these.

The copper tubing will probably be larger than

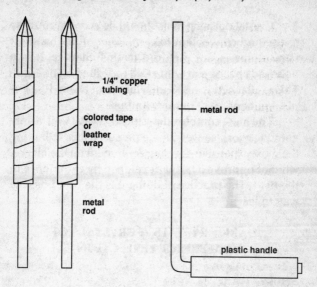

the diameter of the dowsing rods. In order to attach the tips tightly, it may be necessary to use thin copper shims inside the tubing or copper mesh. If this allows them to fit so that they don't slide off, the glue is not needed.

When using the rods it will be necessary to determine what works best for you. For some people a more energetic response is achieved from using the left-handed crystal dowsing rod in the left hand and the right-handed one in the right hand. For others, the reverse works better. You will have to experiment to see which way responds best for you. One rule of procedure does not work for everybody. Crystals and human beings express themselves in unique ways in energy relationship patterns. A joyful expression of love and light helps balance the experience.

Crystal dowsing tools should be economical, easy to use and convenient to carry. One of the handiest pendulums is not pictured in this chapter. It is a polished apache tear with a bell cap glued on one end. This is attached to a 4½-inch length of chain. It's simple, light and easy to carry and use.

The most complex dowsing or crystal tool is only going to work as well as the person using it. Buying the most expensive dowsing equipment on the market will not improve a talent developed by experience in the field. The practice of doing it is the best possible way to learn.

DARK CRYSTALS & CRYSTALS OF IMPERFECT PERFECTION

Smoky Quartz

It's been said that the energy from a smoky quartz crystal can be very intense, that it can be a powerful force for neutralizing negative thoughts and emotions. The clearer specimens of smoky quartz are sometimes used in healing rods with a clear or white quartz crystal in the other end. They help balance the intense energy of the smoky. These can also be used with amethyst or citrine to establish a harmonious energy balance.

The darker, almost completely black, smoky quartz crystals or clusters can be set around the house or added to rock arrangements. This makes a beautiful display while it helps neutralize and disperse negativity. An excellent spot to place smoky quartz crystals is in the potted plants. The crystals and the plants enjoy this.

Dark Crystals

Doorways, phantoms and rainbows can be found in the lighter tinted smoky quartz. Some of these can be used for channeling information or learning, or can even be mounted in power rods that require only one crystal. Either single or double termination crystals will work for this purpose.

Some of the very dark smoky quartz crystals can be used for crystal gazing to receive psychic impressions. This is especially true if they have a shiny black mirror-like surface, such as black obsidian. Polished apache tears fall into the same category.

Sometimes people have a secret fear, combined with a secret fascination, in relation to dark crystals. The fear is unfounded unless it's a secret fear of releasing negative thoughts and emotions. The smoky crystals are white or clear quartz that have been irradiated, either naturally by the Earth or artifically by man. They still radiate the white-light energy.

Amethyst

Amethyst crystals are excellent in combination with other crystals and stones. They provide a balanced and peaceful healing energy. They are not any less powerful or energetic, just more relaxed in their energy radiations. They work well in energy rods with clear, white and smoky quartz crystals. Amethyst crystal clusters set around the home promote a harmonious environment. They also work well in the car, where peace and harmony are frequently needed. They are an excellent choice for personal crystals and can be carried in pockets, purses or on jewelry. Their purple color promotes peace and balance.

Citrine

The gold or brown colors of citrine crystals promote practicality in everyday, down-to-earth matters. They do this while inspiring the highest ideals. They provide a grounding base or foundation of energy that assists in balancing people who are spiritually oriented. People who are spiritual seekers sometimes need a reminder that there is no separation between physical and spiritual expressions except in the mind. Citrine is rarely used in energy rods, but there is no reason why it shouldn't be.

The Crack in the Crystal

Only people call some crystals imperfect. To the best of my knowledge, no other being—spirit, mineral, plant, animal or angel—has ever perceived something the Earth herself created as flawed or imperfect.

The perception of flaws and imperfections seems to be an exclusively human inclination. Is this a reflection of human beings' limited awareness? I think it is. Part of this may be due to our industrial society. People in our society have been conditioned to expect thousands or millions of objects to look exactly the same, stamped out and symmetrical. Nature doesn't work that way. The Universe doesn't create that way either. There are differences in quartz crystals that are not flaws or imperfections, except to narrow-spectrum human vision. The characteristics we humans might consider flaws are part of the energy field transfers that occur throughout Nature.

A crack in a quartz crystal can produce the prism refraction of light we see as a rainbow within a crystal. But there's more than just rainbows from cracks in crystals. The cracks, chips and inclusions determine the energy patterns and frequencies. The so-called flaws may be the characteristic that causes the energy of a certain crystal to be right for you or your particular expression. This is why it is sometimes better to choose a crystal by feel, holding it in your hand before you look at it closely. In crystal work the energy of a crystal is much more important than the appearance.

This also applies to other rock or mineral specimens. Many will be similar in appearance, but it would be very rare to find identical specimens of the same type. Rocks and crystals are seldom what could be called perfect or identical.

I heard a story about a woman who came into a rock shop with a photograph of her friend's rock. She told the shop owner, "I want a rock exactly like this one with green, red, and yellow spots in the same places." Even though the owner explained that Mother Nature doesn't stamp out identical rocks like a factory, the woman refused to accept the explanation.

This shows us that our thinking habits can be blocks to understanding. Like most areas we deal with, individual perception determines our understanding, or lack of understanding, of the mineral kingdom. Mother Earth sees no imperfections in her mineral kingdom. The rocks and crystals are all doing their energy jobs—growing, changing and behaving according to the Earth's pattern. This is more than you can say of the Earth's human kingdom on most days.

14 The Crystal Earth

"Since most people in today's society can't go back to the land, the land will come back to the people."

EARTH ENERGY FLOW TO A NEW AGE EARTH

We as humans sometimes forget to think of the Earth as a moving, growing, changing being. Yet this is what she is. It's obvious during peaks of earthquake or volcanic activity. It's noticeable with large areas of wind and water erosion, and even during forest fires that sweep across large areas. What's not so noticeable is the Earth's land surface flowing in waves, which can vary as much as a foot each day, in a movement similar to the ocean waves, only smoother. This goes on whether we become aware of it or not. The Earth has a geomagnetic field, a constantly moving aura of atmospheric weather patterns. She reaches out into space with her upper atmosphere, complete with ozone layer and radiation belts. This is a very large, alive being we're living on, definitely someone to be taken into consideration.

There are many people concerned about how we are relating to the Earth, who use words such as ecology or environment to describe the Earth systems. It may be time for us to go a step further and wonder what the Earth might be doing to us or with us. The Earth moves and grows in ways that promote a balance of energies. A new human consciousness grows into being at the same time a new Earth consciousness grows into being. People program and charge crystals of the Earth's mineral kingdom, but at the same time, crystal elemental people charge humans during an Earth-human tuning process. The result for Earth and humans is the same—peace and balance for growth and harmony. The energy process of balance stimulates the creation of new forms in the environment, both human-made and Earth-made.

During this process a lot of the Earth moves around, literally, stimulated by human vehicles. Over five billion humans on the planet move large portions of the Earth, thinking it's their idea. This moving involves simple things such as collecting rocks and digging up a garden plot. Human society on a larger scale moves billions of tons of earth, oil, rock, water and gas to build and fuel its constructions. Everything manmade on the planet came from the natural materials the Earth created.

It would be a blow to the egos of humanity to realize their great creations of cities, civilizations, and societies fulfill the same function for the Earth as anthills do. They both move a lot of earth materials from one place to another, which changes the physical and energy balance of the planet. A tremendous amount of the Earth herself is moved around by building highways, buildings, mines or manufactured goods.

This appears to be true throughout history, beginning when humans came to Earth as spirit beings and incarnated in physical bodies. In civilizations of the past, a relatively small population moved a lot of rock and earth. The first materials to be mined and moved were copper, silver, gold, gemstones and crystals. Then larger pieces of earth were moved to various areas. Giant stone blocks were quarried to build cities and pyramid structures at various sites on the Earth.

Who determined where pyramids were built? Was it humans themselves, or humans responding intuitively and instinctively to the guidance from the Earth Mother?

People are again understanding the Earth's energy grid pattern and energy vortexes as the wheel of history comes around. Pyramids of all sizes are being built. Metal, wood and stone is being formed into pyramids from ½-inch quartz crystal jewelry to house-sized wood and stone. At certain times in Earth cycles of thousands of years, people respond to the Earth's impulse to change and balance the planet's entire field of energy. Humans like to believe they thought of it themselves, but the Earth being is, in reality, relaying instructions. Humans respond by constructing forms in the appropriate areas. People are responding to a new cycle of the Earth herself.

What is the Earth responding to? The Father Sun of the solar system is emitting radiations of energy for a cycle change in all the planets. We naturally tend to be Earth oriented, but the energy is affecting the growth consciousness of all our planets.

We often forget to think of planets, solar systems and galaxies as larger beings that are moving into new energy growth patterns. Our Milky Way galaxy, too, is following its path of orbit into a new energy frequency area of the Universe. Our galaxy probably doesn't think of itself, like we do, of entering a New Age. It is moving farther into new energy fields that it hasn't been in before. As it does this, the direct energy communication is channeled on down the line to suns and their solar systems, from planet to planet, moon to moon and asteroid to asteroid. The planets radiate their energy communications to the Earth and the beings that inhabit her—spirit, mineral, animal and human alike.

The channel of energy communication stimulates growth and change in the areas of awareness and expanded consciousness. Everybody is getting the same energy at the same time, in ever increasing amounts. How individual beings handle and adapt to the energy is a personal choice, but each is exposed to new energy growth frequencies to an equal degree. Some people handle the energy more gracefully than others, as can be seen in the six o'clock news.

The flow of energy to the Earth from the Universe is of spiritual essence for human life. There are some enjoyable ways to stimulate this energy while being in balance with it. Hiking and picnicking while rock hunting has a beneficial energy effect on people. Healthy fresh air and exercise are added benefits of finding compatible rocks and crystals to bring home for gardens, yards, planters and terrariums. We find ourselves agreeably helping the Earth move herself in this manner. This brings Nature, beauty and good energy into our home environment.

Rock hunting also allows us to feel the energy of rocks, plants, fish, birds and animals in their natural home environment. Being close to Nature promotes a growing essence of spirit that lets us love ourselves more each day. Bringing home rocks for an outdoor rock garden or an indoor terrarium brings us closer to the Earth with a simple act. It can be as easy as placing a few rocks or crystals in a potted house plant. The contact provides an energy communication with the Earth plant and mineral kingdoms.

The majority of life living on the Earth Mother is not going to speak English or any other human language to us. If we want to communicate and learn about ourselves and Nature, it is in the energy/information language of Nature that we'll do it. Some parts of ourselves, from body cells to higher spirit, do not speak in words. The communication is an energy interchange of energy fields or overlapping dimensions.

This may sound complex and esoteric, but the communication can be as easy as taking care of house plants, a small garden, or flowers in a window box. This can be as fun and relaxing as going for a hike in the country or having a picnic by a river. These activities seem simple and ordinary, but they lead to an understanding of being one with the Earth.

All matter appears to evolve and change in the process of crystallization. This includes rocks, plants, animals and people. Crystallization is the activity of creation by the Universal One, the expression and manifestation of the logical order of creation.

The following quote from Chief Seattle's (Sealth's) speech to the U.S. government in the 1850s finishes up this chapter in the most fitting way I can think of.

> "One thing we know: Our God is also your
> God. The Earth is precious, and to harm the
> Earth is to heap contempt on its creator."

In learning to be one with and love the Earth we live on, we also learn to be one with and love ourselves and all creation.

15　Through the Eye
　　of the Crystal

*"It sometimes seems as if we are trying to defend
something we don't quite have yet, but once we have
it, no defense is necessary."*

SEEING WHAT OUR WORLD CAN BE,
A NEW FUTURE AWARENESS

A world at peace . . . no war.
A world of good health . . . no disease.
A world of plenty . . . no starvation.
A world of prosperity . . . no poverty.
A world with science, art and music developed
　　creatively, as one.
A healthy planet . . . no pollution.
Loving relationships . . . no disharmony.
Freedom and justice for all . . . no oppression.

Visualizing, seeing and being aware that a balanced
world on Earth can be manifested is the first step for a
person taking individual responsibility for bringing it
about. The Earth herself can provide for all of her
children when they decide that a peaceful, abundant
world is what they desire. Ten percent of the world's
population of over five billion people is enough to
balance the planetary environment.

Peace and balance for the planet and its people
must be radiated outward from the minds and hearts

of strong individuals if it's ever to be brought about.

The Universe and the Earth are at peace and in balance with themselves. Peace or balance in this area is anything but a static or stagnant condition. Peace is not calm and unmoving. Humans appear to be the only beings who have the misconception—or misperception—that it is static. At the Universal Energy level of subatomic particles, or with thoughts on a human psionic level, there is constantly rapid change and movement. Particles and energy fields gauge and rebalance the flow of energy creation. Rapid particle interaction, sometimes at the speed of light or faster, is anything but calm and peaceful as we think of it.

The spirit of this constant flux of swirling, interacting energy is the Universal Mind's imagination, visualizing the moving picture of creation, the flow of life. Our spirits can be in harmony with this as we develop, beyond even thoughts, to the instantaneous universal mind picture. With our conscious awareness of the One Source of all, our spirit becomes one with the center of love, peace and harmony that flows through all life and material manifestation. At this point all is one by experience, not just by words or thoughts of being one. This type of energy center within ourselves radiates and communicates outward and inward through all of creation instantly.

An individual visualization, in harmony with the Universal Mind, is like a moving picture with a constant flow. This method of creative visualization appears to be more effective for manifesting peace and harmony for individuals and planets than the static-type mind pictures we use to manifest a new car or a new house.

The moving diagram of spirit projection is also faster than thought transmission, even faster than light. This creative mind motion picture projection can also include vivid colors with sound, smell and touch sensory perceptions for a holistic dimension in balance.

We can positively project a world at peace instead of concentrating on a world without war. The negatives are removed by putting a positive moving picture in its place. The vision of a world at peace is a vision of individuals at peace within ourselves. The nature of peace or conditions of peace include the picture of good health, plenty, prosperity, planetary balance, love, freedom and especially beauty, with science, art and life expressed as one. This vision is being manifested through the eye of the crystal by the essence of ourselves, the spirit of one.

We seek peace in our world because we seek peace within ourselves; yet by being at peace within ourselves, we radiate and project a vision of peace throughout our world.

Being at peace is being One!

16 The Crystal Pipe—
The Vision Became Real

"If you can get into crystals,
You can get into you;
If you can get into you,
You can know yourself;
If you know yourself,
You can be yourself;
If you can be yourself,
YOU ARE IT."

The Crystal Pipe is a product of the new Earth cycle that has just begun. This pipe is based on traditional Native American practices and the science of Universal Energy. It is the most versatile and powerful tool to arise from the inspiration of *Crystal Power*. This quartz crystal and amethyst artifact moves spiritual subatomic particle energy in ways that are awesome. The device was manifested through me with the help of crystal beings from the elemental mineral kingdom. It can be used as an energy field generator, a power rod, a healing rod, an energy hammer (tomahawk), a chakra/aura balancer and more. These pipes are rare (even among crystal people), but they are likely to become the most popular crystal energy tool of the future.

The first use of the Crystal Pipe was in the medicine/prayer/healing circle. Another crystal or crystal rod is used to circle (clockwise) around the amethyst crystal. This is done once for each energy blessing and offering. This covers the whole range of the spirit people, mineral people, plant people, sea people, winged people, four-legged brothers and sisters, two-legged brothers and sisters, the Great Spirit and the Earth Mother. It is helpful to breathe in and out with the breath of the Universe as the pipe is offered to each of the four directions as well as to the Great Spirit and the Earth Mother. For anyone intending this usage, it might be advisable to read two books for an understanding of the traditional practice of the pipe ceremony. These are *Breath of the Invisible* by John Redtail Freesoul, and the standard reference called *The Sacred Pipe*, recorded and edited by Joseph Epes Brown (Black Elk's Account).

Materials and Construction

The Crystal Pipe is constructed using the same materials and methods described in chapter 2 for building the Crystal Rods of Light. Three ¾-inch copper couplings are used for mounting a single termination amethyst crystal, a single termination quartz crystal and a double termination quartz crystal. The crystals should be less than ¾ inch in diameter so that they can be wrapped with a strip of copper screen mesh and glued securely with an instant-bonding glue. The main body of the pipe is formed by gluing a 10½-inch length of ¾-inch diameter copper pipe into one side of a ¾-inch copper tee.

The double termination crystal (already mounted in its coupling) is then glued to the other end of the 10½-inch copper pipe (see diagram). The single termination quartz and amethyst crystals (already mounted in couplings) are attached to the copper tee

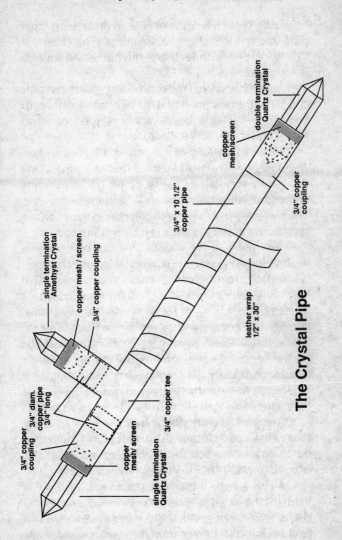

The Crystal Pipe

single termination
Amethyst Crystal

copper mesh / screen

3/4" copper coupling

3/4" copper
coupling

3/4" diam.
copper pipe
3/4" long

copper
mesh/ screen

single termination
Quartz Crystal

3/4" copper tee

double termination
Quartz Crystal

copper
mesh/screen

3/4" x 10 1/2"
copper pipe

3/4" copper
coupling

leather wrap
1/2" x 30"

by gluing ¾-inch lengths of ¾-inch diameter copper pipe into the tee. The main length of pipe (10½″) is then wrapped with leather, which is glued on as it is wrapped.

Like other crystal rods and energy tools, the pipe can be left unwrapped and/or decorated with your favorite gemstones, beads, feathers, gold or silver bands and more, if you desire.

Once completed, the fun and adventure start. Although constructed and used first as a pipe, don't think of this crystal tool as just a pipe. It is an example of the One being the many and the many being One. The two main uses after being an energy pipe are as a crystal power rod and as a crystal healing rod.

Any point of the energy pipe can be used as a healing rod. Try each one until you find one that feels comfortable. In different situations you may use all of them at different times. Use them for visualizing and directing the white-light energy. At the same time, amplify the energy with a feeling of unconditional love and at-oneness. Some people prefer the amethyst for healing, while others prefer the double or single termination quartz. This requires experimenting until you feel at home with the three crystal beings of this tool. There is no substitute for experience with this.

Another recently discovered use is as an aura/chakra balancer. The amethyst tip is pointed at one of the chakra areas while the double termination quartz is pointed at another to connect the energies.

As an energy tomahawk (hammer), this tool is held just the way it sounds. It can be swung in arcs and circles while seeing with the inner eye that it throws a field of Universal Energy from the amethyst and single termination points. Quite a bit of practice is required for this use. This practice is more akin to a martial arts form and technique.

This crystal tool is constantly inspiring new discoveries. One person who held it was reminded of the L-shaped right angle energy patterns related to UFO propulsion, navigation and flight paths using the universal lines of force and energy.

The Crystal Pipe will bring out many more new-old discoveries as individuals of different experience and backgrounds build and use these in creating the "new" world.

17   The One-Minute Crystal Healer

"When using Universal Crystal tools, we are not only connected or interrelated to all things, we are all things."

A thought-particle transmission is faster than light. A moving mind picture visualization is faster than thought through our Ki and the Ki of the crystal. Ki or Chi is the life force energy everywhere. This transmission is not only fast, it's instantaneous, less than a few hundredths of a second. In this space-time frame of reference, 60 seconds is a very long time.

The Universe is a mind information visualization with all things and beings connected. This provides instantaneous information communication. Humans often ignore this factor. However, when humans choose to be conscious of it, they can use this capacity to reach anywhere in the Universe with instant information energy communications and awareness. This awareness, projected with a crystal or crystal tool, is by nature immediate. No time span is required for the action of the mind picture.

USING A CRYSTAL OR CRYSTAL ROD ON YOUR PERSON OR WHILE YOU'RE WALKING, DRIVING OR RIDING.

The most popular size for a personal crystal rod is

½ inch in diameter by 4½ inches in length. My favorite rod uses one double-terminated quartz crystal (chipped and cracked, by the way) with the other end of the copper tube capped with a ½-inch copper cap. This rod is loaded with pieces of natural magnetic lodestone and wrapped with black leather. It also uses the new style mounting, with the crystal in a ½-inch copper coupling that is left unwrapped. This pocket-size rod is just the right size to hold in either hand while comfortably holding the index finger around the crystal with the thumb placed on one of the larger facets. This has proven to be a good grip to use when sitting, driving or walking. It's comfortable for receiving energy or radiating a balanced energy field. It's great for personal use at times when projecting a beam of energy is not required. When using a crystal or crystal rod while traveling by any means of transportation, this grip produces a white-light energy field aura of balance around both the person and the vehicle.

Positive thoughts and feelings of connectedness amplify this aura. An attitude of receptiveness produces the flow of energy that we might need at the time.

This grip on the rod allows the thumb and index finger to be pulled back instantly, exposing the quartz crystal for visualizing and projecting a beam of Universal Energy. A beam of white-light energy can be projected to a reckless driver two car lengths away, or it can be projected half a world away to a war area reported on the car radio. This can be done in a matter of seconds.

In these same few seconds, healing energy can be sent to a passenger sitting next to you who is suffering from a headache. Or, a beam of particle energy can be projected to hold traffic lights on green or yellow for a faster trip across town.

Using a crystal or crystal rod at home, in your garden or yard is just as fast and easy. In less than a minute, healing energy can be sent to a friend or family member who is suffering from a head cold. The same healing energy can be projected to an injured pet or a houseplant that seems to be ailing. All this can be done in seconds.

OTHER USES OF CRYSTALS
IN THE SPACE-TIME OF A MINUTE

The examples of crystal tool uses are frequently given for the crystal rods with clear quartz crystals. This is just a general guideline that can be expanded, developed and improvised upon by individual crystal users. Single or double termination crystals and clusters of all kinds can be used the same way. Cloudy, smoky, rose quartz, amethyst or citrine can all be used for healing in seconds.

The crystal tool can be used in the right or left hand, or both. It can be used for receiving or transmitting. The success of the whole process depends on what you think.

USING A CRYSTAL OR CRYSTAL ROD
IN WAYS THAT ARE PERSONAL,
IMPERSONAL, PLANETARY OR UNIVERSAL

If you frequently use crystals to move Universal Energy for balancing and healing, you are living more and more at one with the Spirit.

The one-minute Crystal Healer seeks to show how fast and easy it is to be at one with the creative energy of the Universe. Your inner awareness grows with healing and balance. This in turn affects healing and balance on the planetary Earth Mother. This spirit energy movement radiates throughout the solar system, the galaxy and the Universe. It is the constant energy of growth, self and source. One simple act of love and energy towards a plant in the garden enriches the quality of life in all of the world.

What we send out as one-minute crystal healers returns to us multiplied hundreds of times over. We are also healing ourselves with the Spirit of One. Being at one with the Universal for even one minute per day makes a difference in the amount of good energy flowing around the Earth. This works if we send the energy or receive it ourselves. We can enjoy the healing energy by just sitting for a minute holding a crystal or crystal tool. Just looking at the beauty of a crystal or touching one can form a field of beneficial energy.

The one-minute crystal healing experience may appear to be the "fast food" of the crystal world. Since now is the only time we live in, and all creation is everywhere and instantly connected, the one-minute experience is practical for now. Many times in our modern self-created world, we don't or won't take the one hour, half hour, or 15 minutes for meditation or affirmation that some spiritual practices ask for. A minute of time can usually be found by even the busiest of people during the busiest day. That one minute can be the one that makes a difference. What we can think of, we can do . . . right now!

ONE-MINUTE CRYSTAL HEALING TOOLS

The most convenient of these are

1. Crystals or crystal clusters by themselves
2. Pocket- or purse-sized crystal rods
3. Crystal jewelry such as pendants, ankle brace-

lets, necklaces, earrings, rings, bracelets, pins and tie tacks

4. Crystal wristbands
5. Crystal (cloth) headbands
6. Crystal ankle wallets
7. Car crystals and healing stones
8. Crystal pendulums

All of these are easy to carry and use. The crystals, clusters, crystal rods and jewelry are familiar items to most of us. The crystal and healing stone wristbands, cloth headbands and ankle wallets are newer additions to crystal work, so a diagram is included for general guidelines and helpful hints.

Sports Wrist Bands
With Quartz Crystals in pockets

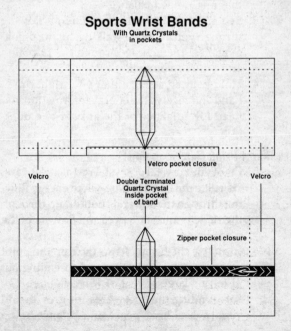

Velcro

Velcro pocket closure

Double Terminated
Quartz Crystal
inside pocket
of band

Velcro

Zipper pocket closure

Ankle wallets are frequently found in small mail-order gift catalogues. The wristbands, with or without zipper pockets, are usually available in sports or sporting goods stores that cater to joggers. The elasticized cloth material about two inches wide for making headbands is available in most fabric stores.

ONE-MINUTE CRYSTAL HEALING PRACTICES

Healing Yourself

1. Sit quietly for a minute, feeling the peaceful energy field from your crystal energize your aura while being at one with all.
2. See the energy beam from your crystal pouring healing energy into any area of your body that might need balance.
3. See and feel the Universal Energy flowing through you as you're walking, hiking or jogging. Feel the energy through the crystal in and around yourself.
4. Hold your crystal in either your right or left hand and receive the energy information you need for guidance or the answer to a question.

Healing a Plant, Garden or Yard

5. Point your crystal or crystal rod at a plant and visualize the beam of blue-white energy flowing through the soil and roots on up through the stalk, branches, leaves and flowers of the plant being.
6. Visualize the beam of energy from the point of your crystal projecting and spreading out to form a large sphere of white-light energy surrounding the entire area for growth and vitality. Feel love, peace and balance and a

sense of oneness with the Earth at the same time you are doing this.

Healing the Earth

7. Visualize the crystal energy spreading out to form a sphere or aura of good energy surrounding the Earth.

8. See the beam of energy from the point of your crystal flowing out across or through the Earth to a specific area that needs help. Feel love and a sense of oneness with the Earth Mother while you do this.

9. See the beam of energy reaching across the Earth to a person who is making an environmental decision—see it working for the good of the Earth Mother.

Healing an Animal

10. See the beam of energy going to the animal and balancing the energy field for life and joy with a feeling of love for our brother or sister being.

11. See the beam of energy flowing into the afflicted area, balancing and removing blockages to restore or promote good health with a feeling of love.

Healing Another Person

12. See the energy flowing through the point of the crystal to the person's aura, near or far away, bringing balance and well-being to that person with a feeling of unconditional love.

13. See the beam of energy pouring into the afflicted area of the person's body, clearing blockages, restoring balance for good health.

> See the energy flowing into the person's head and heart area, bringing good energy to heal negative thoughts and emotions that might have caused the imbalance and affliction.

There's something that happens for a minute while we are using crystals and crystal tools. It happens for much longer periods when we are engaged in building and creating crystal devices. This "something" is within ourselves—it is awareness. It is not the result of meditation or philosophical practice. It is not the result of creative visualization or the mental gymnastics we do by our thinking self or thoughts. It is something that happens when working with crystals.

I thought crystals were just a passing fad. After a decade and a half . . . well, that's what I get for thinking. This "thing" is more than just awareness of what is around us or awareness of self.

This thing is beyond self. This thing is ONE.

STAY IN TOUCH

On the following pages you will find listed, with their current prices, some of the books and tapes now available on related subjects. Your book dealer stocks most of these, and will stock new titles in the Llewellyn series as they become available. We urge your patronage.

To obtain a FREE COPY of our latest full CATALOG of New Age books, tapes, videos, crystals, products and services, just write to the address below. In each 80 page catalog sent out bimonthly, you will find articles, reviews, the latest information on New Age topics, a listing of news and events, and much more. It is an exciting and informative way to stay in touch with the New Age and the world. The first copy will be sent free of charge and you will continue receiving copies as long as you are an active customer. You may also subscribe to *The Llewellyn New Times* by sending a $2.00 donation ($7.00 for Canada & Mexico, and $20.00 for overseas). Order your copy of *The Llewellyn New Times* today!

The Llewellyn New Times
P.O. Box 64383-Dept. 726, St. Paul, MN 55164

TO ORDER BOOKS AND PRODUCTS ON THE FOLLOWING PAGES:

If your book dealer does not carry the titles and products listed on the following pages, you may order them directly from Llewellyn. Just write us a letter. Please add $2 for postage and handling for orders of $10 and under. Orders over $10 require $3.50 postage and handling. (USA and in US funds). UPS Delivery: We ship UPS whenever possible. Delivery guaranteed. Provide your street address as UPS does not deliver to P.O. Boxes; UPS to Canada requires a $50 minimum order. Allow 4-6 weeks for delivery. Orders outside the USA and Canada: Airmail—add $5 per book; add $3 for each non-book item (tapes, etc.); add $1 per item for surface mail.

Send orders to:

LLEWELLYN PUBLICATIONS
P.O. Box 64383-726
St. Paul, MN 55164-0383, U.S.A.

CRYSTAL POWER
by Michael G. Smith

This is an amazing book, for what it claims to present—with complete instructions and diagrams so that YOU can work them yourself—is the master technology of ancient Atlantis: psionic (mind-controlled and life-energized machines) devices made from common quartz crystals!

Learn to easily construct an "Atlantean" Power Rod that can be used for healing or a weapon; or a Crystal Headband stimulating psychic powers; or a Time and Space Communications Generator; operated purely by your mind.

These crystal devices seem to work only with the disciplined mind power of a human operator, yet their very construction seems to start a process of growth and development, a new evolutionary step in the human psyche that bridges mind and matter.

Does this "re-discovery" mean that we are living, now, in the New Atlantis? Have these Power Tools been re-invented to meet the needs of this prophetic time? Are Psionic Machines the culminating Power To the People to free us from economic dependence on fossil fuels and smokestack industry?

This book answers "yes" to all these questions, and asks you to simply build these devices and put them to work to help bring it all about.

0-87542-725-1, 288 pgs., illus., 5¼ x 8, softcover $9.95

CRYSTAL HEALING: The Next Step
by Phyllis Galde

Discover the further secrets of quartz crystal! Now modern research and use have shown that crystals have even more healing and therapeutic properties than has been realized. Learn why polished, smoothed crystal is better to use to heighten your intuition, improve creativity and for healing.

Learn to use crystals for reprogramming your subconscious to eliminate problems and negative attitudes that prevent success. Here are techniques that people have successfully used—not just theories.

This book reveals newly discovered abilities of crystal now accessible to all, and is a sensible approach to crystal use. *Crystal Healing* will be your guide to improve the quality of your life and expand your consciousness.

0-87542-246-2, 224 pgs., illus., mass market $3.95

LLEWELLYN'S QUARTZ CRYSTALS

Beautiful natural quartz crystals. Llewellyn now has a good supply of crystals that were mined in Arkansas. They come in two sizes and are high-energy crystals. They are all single terminated and are clear at the point. We look them over before we send them to you so you are guaranteed of getting one of the finest crystals available.

Crystal A, approx. 2 inches long $10.00 + $1.00 postage

LLEWELLYN'S GEMSTONES

Healers and magicians have always used special stones in their work. We are now offering some of these special stones, each endowed by legend and ancient tradition with specific powers.

GEM•PAK I contains one each of the following four stones: Amethyst, Bloodstone, Carnelian, and Tiger Eye.

GEM•PAK II contains one each of the following four stones: Rose Quartz, Lace Agate, Sodalite, and Apache Tear Drop.

GEM•CARD contains Amethyst, Bloodstone, Tiger Eye, Carnelian, Smokey Quartz, Aventurine, Rose Quartz, Apache Tear Drop, Tourmalinated Quartz, Sodalite.

GEM•PAK I / $5.00   GEM•PAK II / $5.00   GEM•CARD / $7.95

LLEWELLYN GEM•BAG

Llewellyn's Gem•Bag is an attractive suede drawstring pouch containing 15 different polished gemstones for healing, well-being, and good luck. Each stone has its own special energy, its unique energies and vibrations from its place of origin. They share their gifts and energies with you. Each of these medicine bags comes with complete instructions and descriptions of the gems. Gems include Amazonite, Amethyst, Aventurine, Blue Lace Agate, Carnelian, Crazy Lace Agate, Jade, Moonstone, Petrified Wood, Rhodonite, Rose Quartz, Apache Tear Drop, Snowflake Obsidian, Tiger Eye, and Unikite.

GEM•BAG   **$9.95 each**

CRYSTAL AWARENESS
by Catherine Bowman

For millions of years, crystals have been waiting for people to discover their wonderful powers. Today they are used in watches, computer chips and communication devices. But there is also a spiritual, holistic aspect to crystals.

Crystal Awareness will teach you everything you need to know about crystals to begin working with them. It will also help those who have been working with them to complete their knowledge. Topics include: Crystal Forms, Colored and Colorless Crystals, Single Points, Clusters and Double Terminated Crystals, Crystal and Human Energy Fields, The Etheric and Spiritual Bodies, Crystals as Energy Generators, Crystal Cleansing and Programming, Crystal Meditation, The Value of Polished Crystals, Crystals and Personal Spiritual Growth, Crystals and Chakras, How to Make Crystal Jewelry, The Uses for Crystals in the Future, Color Healing, Programming Crystals with Color, Compatible Crystals and Metals, Several Crystal Healing Techniques, including The Star of David Healing.

Crystal Awareness is destined to be the guide of choice for people who are beginning their investigation of crystals.
0-87542-058-3, 200 pgs., mass market, illus., $3.95

THE MESSAGE OF THE CRYSTAL SKULL
By Alice Bryant & Phyllis Galde

The most fascinating, mysterious artifact ever discovered by mankind. Thousands of years old, yet it is beyond the capabilities of today's technology to duplicate it. Those who have touched the skull or seen photographs of it claim increased psychic abilities and purification. Read this book and discover how this mystical quartz crystal skull can benefit you and all of humankind. Famed biocrystallographer Frank Dorland shares his research of the skull.
0-87542-092-3, 200 pgs., mass market, illus., photos $3.95

EARTH POWER: TECHNIQUES OF NATURAL MAGIC
by Scott Cunningham

Magick is the art of working with the forces of Nature to bring about necessary, and desired, changes. The forces of Nature—expressed through Earth, Air, Fire and Water—are our "spiritual ancestors" who paved the way for our emergence from the pre-historic seas of creation. Attuning to, and working with these energies in magick not only lends you the power to affect changes in your life, it also allows you to sense your own place in the larger scheme of Nature. Using the "Old Ways" enables you to live a better life, and to deepen your understanding of the world about you. The tools and powers of magick are around you, waiting to be grasped and utilized. This book gives you the means to put Magick into your life, shows you how to make and use the tools, and gives you spells for every purpose.

0-87542-121-0, 176 pgs., 5¼ x 8, illus., softcover $6.95

CUNNINGHAM'S ENCYCLOPEDIA OF CRYSTAL, GEM & METAL MAGIC
by Scott Cunningham

It is very rare that a book becomes a classic. Just such a book is *Cunningham's Encyclopedia of Crystal, Gem and Metal Magic*.

Here you will find the most complete information anywhere on the magical qualities of over 75 crystals and gemstones as well as several metals. The information includes: the Energy of each gem, crystal or metal; the planet(s) which rule(s) the crystal, gem or metal; the magical element (Air, Earth, Fire, Water) associated with the gem, crystal or metal; the deities associated with each; and the Tarot card associated with each; the magical powers each crystal, metal and stone are believed to possess. Also included is a complete description of how to use each gemstone, crystal and metal for magical purposes.

This is the book everyone will want to have! This is the book everyone will be quoting. This will be the classic on the subject.

0-87542-126-1, 240 pgs., 6 x 9, color, softcover $12.95

PSYCHIC POWER
by Charles Cosimano

Although popular in many parts of the world, *Radionics* machines have had little application in America, *UNTIL NOW!* Charles Cosimano's book, *Psychic Power*, introduces these machines to America with a new purpose: to increase your psychic powers! Using the easy, step-by-step instructions, and for less than a $10.00 investment, you can build a machine which will allow you to read other people's minds, influence their thoughts, communicate with their dreams and be more successful when you do divinations such as working with Tarot cards or Pendulums.

Read the book, build the devices and find out for yourself.
0-87542-097-4, 224 pages, mass market, illus. **$3.95**

PSIONIC POWER
by Charles Cosimano

Can a machine really amplify one's psychic powers? In his book *Psychic Power* (formerly *Psionics 101*), Charles Cosimano showed thousands how to build simple, effective and inexpensive radionic devices. Now he's back with a new book that propels radionics into a new decade.

Radionics fuses ancient traditions and modern technology into a workable whole. Cosimano shows how radionic devices can be used for such tasks as

- Measuring the aura
- Controlling functions of the chakras
- Thought control
- Self-defense

The author also includes brand-new diagrams for psychic amplifiers and plans for a crystal transmitter. *Psionic Power* offers readers fascinating insight into techniques of chakra balancing, healing, psychic self-defense and more.
0-87542-096-6, 214 pgs., mass market, illus. **$3.95**

LLEWELLYN ORDER FORM
LLEWELLYN PUBLICATIONS
P.O. Box 64383-726, St. Paul, MN 55164-383

You may use this form to order any of the Llewellyn books or services listed in this publication.

Give Title, Author, Order Number and Price.

_____

_____

_____

_____

_____

_____

_____

Postage and handling: include $2.00 for orders under $10.00 or $3.50 for orders over $10.00. We ship UPS so please use street address. MN residents add 6% sales tax. Outside USA, add $5.00 per book. You may charge on your ☐ Visa, ☐ MC, or ☐ American Express.

Account Number_____

Exp. Date_____Phone_____

Signature_____

Name_____

Address_____

City, State, Zip_____

CHARGE CARD ORDERS (minimum $15.00) may call 1-800-THE-MOON (in USA and Canada) during regular business hours, Monday-Friday, 8:00 am-9:00 pm, CST. Other questions please call 612-291-1970.

☐ **Please send me your FREE CATALOG!**